HOW
TO *Say*
NO

KICK THE DISEASE
TO PLEASE

CORINNE SWEET

Acorn Independent Press

To C the C
For being there throughout

Contents

Acknowledgments

Many thanks to my brilliant agent, Jane Graham Maw, of Graham Maw Christie; to Leila Green of Acorn Independent Press; to Ben Walker for excellent research and for keeping things afloat; to Johnny McKeown for fun, advice and support; and to Clara, for simply being wonderful. And finally, thanks to the Keedees for their midnight solace.

PART ONE

Why Can't You
Say 'No'?

1

Do you say 'yes' when you want to say 'no'?

Have you ever said 'yes' to something or someone and regretted it afterwards?

Perhaps you have felt you 'ought' to work late when asked or 'must' do a favour for a friend? Maybe you feel you 'should' go home and visit family, particularly on high days and holidays, when you don't really want to? Or you might be the kind of person who spends a lot of your time, energy and life 'double-guessing' what other people want or need? When someone hints at something that needs doing, or even when they ask you directly, 'no' is just not in your vocabulary. You feel put on the spot, and instead of being straight and saying, 'I'm sorry, I can't help you,' or 'I'd love to, but I don't have the time,' you find yourself telling little white lies, making excuses, even creating complex stories, to get out of what feels like an impossible situation. I know someone who always has a bad headache when she doesn't want to go out with a particular friend; and someone else gets flu every time it's the weekend to go home and visit his widowed father. The truth is: *they don't want to do these things, but can't find a way of being direct about it with the people concerned.* They simply can't say 'no'.

Oughts, shoulds and double-guessing

If the above is true of you, then you're caught in the emotional thicket of all the oughts, shoulds and double-guessing that can make life very difficult. The worst part about it - or at least the most confusing - is that at the time of saying 'yes' you may well even convince yourself that you really do want to do whatever it is you've agreed to. In fact, you're so much on automatic that it's hard to stop and think what you really want for yourself at all. What's more, the times when you don't want to do something but you still do it create so much tension and bad feeling within you that you can end up feeling grudging, even bitter and resentful. You might even pick a fight. I've done this myself many times: I've said, 'Yes, that's fine, I'll do it,' almost through clenched teeth, and afterwards have berated myself with 'WHY on earth did I agree to that?'

Happy Helper Habit

When I started talking to people about this book I had an overwhelming response from women, and some men, who cried, 'Oh my God, that's me. I could do with reading your book.' The self-confessed appeasers were more than happy to help — naturally. I call it the Happy Helper Habit. Obviously, we all want to have successful and happy lives, we want to be liked, even loved, we want to be fit, active and attractive, but more than all of that, we want to *belong*. So when a request is made (or hinted at), even a fairly impossible one, we can find ourselves saying 'yes' and twist, even contort, ourselves trying to help in the hope that it will bring some, if not all, of the above rewards. Then we're disappointed when it doesn't change things dramatically, but ever hopeful (we often don't learn our lesson) we find ourselves slipping into Happy Helper mode the very next time someone says, 'Could you just... ?' or 'Would you ... ?' So why is saying 'no' so difficult for some people? Tina's story is a good example of the seductive pull of trying to be helpful to all.

'I can't say no': Tina's 'Happy Helper' story

Tina, thirty-five, a hairdresser, is married with two children under five and works part-time in a small seaside community. She works one day a week in a salon and her husband, Simon, works full-time as a boat chandler. The problem is, Tina keeps giving people free haircuts when she doesn't really want to. 'It started with giving a haircut as a birthday present to a friend,' explains Tina, 'then I did her husband and her two kids.' On her days at home with the kids, Tina has anything from one to six people visit - and she cuts their hair for nothing or for a couple of pounds. 'It all started as doing people a favour, but now I feel trapped,' she says. 'I call myself a Happy Helper, but it doesn't make me happy, really.' Recently, she offered a perm to a friend for £15 because she felt sorry for her. After she had finished three hours of hairdressing her friend said she only had £10. 'I smiled and said that's fine,' admits Tina, 'but when I closed the door I felt drained and upset. It felt good doing her a favour, but afterwards I felt resentful and exhausted.' Even on her wedding day, Tina found herself doing everybody's hair and her own last. 'I wanted to feel special, but ended up feeling as if everybody else was the bride, not me.'

So why does Tina say 'yes' when she really wants to say 'no'? 'I live in a small community and I'm worried if I say "no" it will offend people and people will talk,' explains Tina. 'I also don't really value myself, I suppose, and think, "Ah, they haven't got much money, I must help them," but it drives my husband wild, especially when I work weekends, and he says, "You're doing them favours, what favours are they doing you?"' Tina agrees she has boxed herself in with her Happy Helper Habit: "I've got sucked into it all and I do want to change and be able to say "no", but I just don't know how.'

Why is it so hard to say 'no'?

'No' is a small but powerful word. A shake of the head, an assertion of the negative: 'no'. Yet, it eludes Tina. It may elude you, too. 'No' may seem simple to say, but, boy, has it been drummed into most of us from an early age that 'no' is virtually impossible to say nicely. It's rude to say 'no'. It is not polite. It offends. Nearly every person I interviewed for this book said, 'I don't want to offend other people,' or 'People won't like me,' or 'I don't want to be rude,' or 'It's just not nice.' One of the first lessons we teach our children is to say 'Yes, please' with 'No, thank you' a shy second. However, we learn fairly soon that refusal can cause offence: we teach our children to take a piece of Aunt Mildred's dreadful rock cake (it really is made of rocks) out of politeness. It may sit untouched on your plate, but it's not been refused and therefore no offence has been caused.

Cultural reasons for not saying 'no'

There are cultural reasons which make us feel we can't say 'no'. For instance, within some cultural groups it will cause offence not to try a particular delicacy or not to remove your shoes on entering a house. If you ignore cultural customs this can, indeed, cause a serious upset. It is usually a rule of thumb: 'When in Rome, do as the Romans do' - so you should visit other countries, cultures or households with an open mind, which can lead you to saying 'yes' rather than 'no'. For instance, if you don't drink alcohol and you are offered wine, you might take a glass, even a sip, as a sign of respect; conversely, you may expect wine but be offered tea instead. I was once offered a jar of cranberries while visiting Russia, by a family who had little money and virtually no food. The cranberries represented a year's harvest and would have bought them food and essentials at the market. I was the honoured guest and I was offered an extraordinarily valuable gift. I felt guilty as hell, but took the generous gift with grace, knowing it would offend deeply to refuse. A blunt 'no' in this kind of situation would have made enemies, rather than friends.

Religious reasons for not saying 'no'

Some religions teach people to be stoical, to put others first and to turn the other cheek. Others hold martyrdom as a model for good behaviour. Rose, a fifty-eight-year-old nurse brought up as a strict Roman Catholic in Ireland, told me, 'I saw my mother absorb my father's anger and bad behaviour and act like a saint. She never said "no" to him, she just took it on the chin and dealt with us children. I used to think, "Why doesn't she stand up to him?" but she used to say it was her cross to bear.' Not surprisingly, in her own life Rose has found it hard to say 'no' to fairly abusive partners and has taken on too much at work, too much responsibility in her family and neighbourhood, because the role model she had was one of uncomplaining self-sacrifice, even martyrdom.

Similarly, Carolyn, a twenty-three-year-old musician, was brought up strictly by parents in the Salvation Army, and remembers, 'It was rules, rules, rules at home. I felt like I could never get anything right. "No" wasn't allowed at all. We had to have good manners, clear our plates, only speak when spoken to and not watch TV. I had to say "yes" to any request, like washing up or playing the violin, as not to meant I got a smack or was sent to my room. I can't say "no" now in my own life, which means I sulk and get very pent up with anger.'

Obviously, religion is a very important framework for many families and there are plenty of good aspects to religious teachings. However, some people rebel and react against their over-strict religious upbringings, especially when they are not allowed self-expression or dissent. The messages of putting others first, not being selfish and always thinking of others before yourself can actually make it difficult to stand your ground in adult life, especially if your family of origin was not a particularly happy one (see Chapter 3 for more on this).

Social reasons for not saying 'no'

For most of us, life has sped up to inhuman proportions in the twenty-first century: we live 24/7 pressured lives with few real breaks or respites from pressure. With low job security it's extremely hard to turn off the mobile phone, answerphone, TV or Internet. We might just miss something or someone important: an opportunity, a promotion, a new lover or friend, even life itself. The pressure to meet all demands from all quarters has never been so intense, so it means it can be extremely hard to say 'no' today. When we try to please everyone all the time, we get very stressed as a consequence, and that stress is detrimental, especially long term, to our mental and physical health. Guy, twenty-eight, who manages a branch of a chain of fast-food restaurants, says, 'I have to please the customer, I have to please my boss, I have to keep to company and government regulations and I have to make sure the staff are happy. I end up completely squeezed in the middle and sometimes I feel I'm going crazy on the job.' Stress also blights our capacity for happiness. It also explains why 'road rage' and other similar 'rages' are increasingly common (have you noticed what a short fuse so many people seem to have these days?). Society has become an emotional pressure cooker and, after a day trying to meet impossible demands while being a 'yes' man or woman, something has to blow.

Superwoman has a lot to answer for

One of the first steps is to acknowledge that you have limits. That you are human. That you are not superwoman or superman. With the myth of superwoman hanging over our heads today, many women, like Tina the hairdresser, are living impossible lives, or at least *trying* to. The work-life balance is a fabulous idea, but it doesn't really exist in practice for the majority. Most women want to work, even part-time (we need to, to keep sane, and, of course, we need the money), but we feel guilty about being 'selfish' or worry what the effect will be on the kids, if we have them. So we try to squeeze in more and more.

Novelist and mother of two Diana Appleyard, explains the modern woman's archetypal dilemma (it's also the subject of her novel, *Out of Love*, published by Black Swan): 'I find it hard to say "no", which is typical of women of my generation. I feel guilty that I have an independent life and work, and that my career is important to me. It's like an indulgence, which takes me away from the traditional role of wife and mother. So I overcompensate by not saying "no" to anybody, not to my husband, my children, my work or my family. I end up tying myself in knots trying to do it all to an impossible degree of perfection. So I end up feeling utterly exhausted and resentful trying to juggle it all.'

Spinning plates or flat spin?

Women often describe their lives as feeling like a crazy circus act where several plates are set spinning on the end of long poles. Trying to keep all the plates spinning, without dropping them, is an ambidextrous skill demanding every fibre of a modern multitasking woman's attention. However, blink for a second and the plates spin out of control, flying in all directions. Once out of kilter, it's easy to end up in a flat spin instead. Recent research shows that plate-spinning women, like Diana, are still doing most of the housework, running the home, organising the social life, doing the house-beautifying, looking after the pets and managing the finances, while working and looking after the children. Part-time women workers can get very demoralised that all their hard-earned income goes straight out on to paying for childcare, with little left over for themselves. Women also still often end up responsible for elderly parents, as they live longer today and there is an expectation that family members will look after them - or at least help them work out what they want to do - as they age. This can take up a great deal of time, effort, money and family resources, which is fine if there is a good reciprocal relationship, but can be stressful if the relationship is strained and/or there are step-families involved. The desire to be competent and helpful, however, can lead to agreeing to help when it doesn't really suit either party particularly.

The superwoman myth can also affect women's health and well-being adversely. They are expected to remain or become young, slim, attractive, wrinkle-free and sexy, even after having children, and this pressure can lead them to be on constant yo-yo diets, to develop eating disorders or to feel bad about their bodies and themselves. Many women end up saying 'no' to health and healthy eating and living in favour of starving or bingeing and using cigarettes to suppress appetite, and alcohol or drugs to numb feelings, in the hope of ending up like a Victoria Beckham or Beyoncé-type celebrity. Of course, it's a fairly impossible task for most 'ordinary' women, who don't have a bevy of personal trainers and assistants and pots of money to help them achieve a glossy, well-honed look. We lesser mortals need to say 'no' to impossible ideals.

Superman has a lot to answer for, too...

Men tend to work inhumanly long hours in the UK, and they certainly work the longest hours in Europe. Work stress is taking its toll on men's health and well-being in terms of stress-related illnesses, such as lung disease, heart disease and cancer, and one of the reasons is that men simply can't say 'no' to all the demands made on them, as men. At work, their in-trays get larger, the competition is fiercer, while job security is lower than ever. 'Change is here to stay,' explains Professor Cary Cooper, 50th Anniversary Professor of Organisational Psychology and Health at Alliance Management Business School (Alliance MBS). Change is, in fact, one of the monumental stress factors of our time. There's no such thing as a 'job for life' these days, so it is harder to say 'no' to a boss who is asking you to jump through hoops of fire. Men who separate or divorce have to provide money for their ex-family, as well as for their next family and/or step-children, and this often puts them in a financial vice. With one in two marriages failing, a lot of men are struggling with their financial responsibilities, which again makes it harder to say 'no' when extra work is on the cards.

At home, women rightly expect more from men today, too. It clearly is important that men should be more involved with childcare and home-making as well as being a perfect DIY guru and gardening god. However, men often feel under pressure to wash up and nappy-change, when all they really want to do is chill out in front of the TV, lay a perfect patio or plant a potato patch. This doesn't let men off the hook, and they certainly should pull their weight on the domestic front, but it may explain their reluctance to do non-traditional chores. Women also expect more satisfaction sexually today, and men, however pooped out at the end of a hard day, are expected to rise to the occasion. The expectation is that men will always say 'yes' when sex is on offer and their very masculinity is on the block if they say 'no' to a partner; but they may well be too stressed to 'perform', which in turn creates more stress and distress in bed and, therefore, in the relationship.

Psychological reasons for not saying 'no'

As well as the cultural, religious, social and gender issues which make us say 'yes' when we don't want to, there are myriad psychological reasons for not saying 'no': this is what this book mainly focuses on.

The Four 'Yes' Hooks

There seem to be four main emotional reasons which make us say 'yes' instead of 'no'. I see them as hooks we get caught on:

1 You want to be NICE.
2 You want to be LIKED/LOVED/RESPECTED.
3 You FEAR LOSING friends, lovers, family, work and social position, success, money, material goods.
4 You feel you DON'T HAVE THE RIGHT TO SAY NO.

Too nice for your own good?

Some people are driven by the desire to be considered 'nice' at all costs. It's a powerful 'yes' hook, as we saw above. Being nice comes down to culture, class and life experience but, more likely, it's down to a deep psychological need to be accepted. Overly nice people are usually secretly *desperate* to be liked, even loved, by *absolutely everyone* (which is, of course, impossible and also not particularly desirable). They spend time and energy anticipating, even meeting, other people's needs to the detriment of their own. At the same time, they find it almost impossible to say what they want - or even know what they want. They expect others to be as considerate and thoughtful as they are, and can be very disappointed when they're not.

The book *The Nice Factor Book: Are You Too Nice for Your Own Good?* by authors and therapists Robin Chandler and Jo Ellen Grzyb explains eloquently how being too nice can, in fact, blight your life. '"Nice" is at the end of the spectrum of possible behaviour where people are ineffective, invisible, adaptive and powerless,' explain the authors. 'We do not think being nice is wrong. It can be a lovely way to behave: it can mean being sensitive, thoughtful, caring, understanding and attentive to the needs of others. There are times when it is very important to be accommodating, pleasant and agreeable.' However - and as in the case of Tina the hairdresser, who we met earlier - being nice 'becomes a problem when you are too attentive, too thoughtful, too agreeable, too understanding. It becomes a problem when you don't feel you have a choice in how you behave and are therefore nice when you would rather act differently. Then it usually means impotence, unspoken frustration, low-level depression and a real sense of something being not quite right.'

Low self-esteem and lack of self-confidence

'Something being not quite right' indicates how being 'too nice' can also be a cover for low self-esteem and a lack of self-confidence. 'I don't think I'm that good or that I deserve what I really want,' explains Tina. When she had her children, Tina's wildest dream was to stay home with them and work just one day a week. Instead, she is slaving away, for free, on the days she is at home. Why? It's as if she has no right over her own life, no power to decide what she wants. It also points to her feeling that her own skills and time have no real value and can be given away freely to others (who obviously need more help than she does). Indeed, Tina, like many of us who can't say 'no', is driven by all sorts of unconscious motivations. At root, she feels unworthy, not good enough, as if other people have the right to take from her whatever she has to give. 'I do get a buzz from doing haircuts for free, I feel moved by people's sob stories, but sometimes I do feel terribly taken for granted,' she admits.

Tina is desperately trying to boost her low self-esteem by buying people's gratitude. Unfortunately, while people are taking advantage of her need for validation, her self-esteem soars during the moments that the lucky free clients say 'thank you', only to plummet once they go out the door. Her lack of self-confidence is keeping her caught on the Four 'Yes' Hooks, so she continues to say yes' when she wants to say 'no'. Does this ring any bells for you? Have you got the Happy Helper Habit in any way?

How can you break the Happy Helper Habit?

To break the Happy Helper Habit you have to decide that your own life is important and that you can choose how your time and energy is spent. We will return to this theme throughout the book; however, there are some simple steps to start with here.

If you, like Tina above, are in a situation where you are helping too much or appeasing because you feel sorry for people or want to be liked, then ask yourself:

- What would happen if you continued, because you wanted to, but set firm conditions, such as being paid, time limits, etc.?

or, even:

- What would happen if you said to them, 'I've decided not to do this anymore'?

My hunch is this would feel very awkward, especially at first. If you have got yourself into a pickle with somebody or something, you have to disengage yourself in order to sort things out. Once a relationship or a situation has fallen into a pattern, it can feel or actually be very difficult, although not impossible, to shift the ground-rules. For instance, when you go out with a particular friend, you always spend more than them because they're always broke. However, you're beginning to feel resentful at paying more, but you don't know how to broach the subject, especially if you feel sorry for them. It's also embarrassing to talk about money and can feel difficult to raise the issue of how much you pay when you're out together. This might make you feel really mean, so you might start avoiding them rather than face the issue. Rather than say, 'Sorry, I can't pay again tonight, could we talk about how much we spend,' you'd rather absent yourself and risk losing a friend instead.

Keeping people out

People who say 'yes' all the time, instead of 'no' when they want to, are not usually very happy and not very happy with themselves, either. Life can feel burdensome and other people can feel overwhelming: it can all seem too much. It's sad to think you might feel you have to keep people out of your life, instead of learning how to handle them well. The problem is, if you can't say 'no' you probably feel you'd rather carry on as you are instead of changing things. However, continuing as you are and not being able to set clear psychological boundaries means that you'll end up resentful. However, you can choose to do something else, other than withdraw.

Psychological patterns

The good news is, you can choose to try to get rid of the pattern of behaviour, rather than getting rid of the person. You need to distinguish between patterns and people: patterns are not the same as people, they are guiding psychological forces, often hidden from our conscious minds, which we need to analyse and understand in order to change. People are often at the mercy of their patterns, but you can often see the person, quite clearly, hidden underneath their patterns, if you make an effort to look. Challenge their pattern and your friend may well admit they always turn up without cash - and you can start talking about the problem. If your friend defends their pattern to the hilt, then maybe it's time to talk about the relationship and how you feel about their behaviour.

Believe me, I know about this subject, inside out, which is why I am extremely pleased to be writing this book. I have found, not only when I agreed to write this book but as I have been writing it, that I have had to catch myself several times - because, dear reader, I have indeed been someone who has found it extremely hard to say 'no'. Especially to people I care about. Especially to things that matter. Especially when I convince myself I can do everything, all the time, to a perfect standard. So this book is written from the heart and I welcome you on a psychological journey with me to discover just why we can end up agreeing to things, helping others, taking care, doing chores, working late — *when we really don't want to.* Also, why, if we do succeed in saying 'no' to someone or something, it can unleash a torrent of anxiety, guilt, anger, even self-loathing and fear.

Power of decision

If you feel other people are the problem, you may well feel that they should stop putting pressure on you. Well, there's an important point to note here: life and all its pressures, family and love problems, the needs of children and the elderly, work and health crises, and friends in need *will not go away.* The only thing that can change is *you* — in your attitude and behaviour towards these everyday pressures of life. Of course, I would like to have a magic wand, worthy of Harry Potter, to change our behaviour in the twinkling of an eye. I fantasise about being suddenly different, free of repetitive patterns which drive me (and others who know me) nuts, but I know from experience, not only for myself but from counselling and psychotherapy, that I can't give anyone a magic spell to make things better overnight. I wish I could. *Kerpow, now you can say 'no', stand your ground and feel totally comfortable about it.* I'd love to be able to do that, of course, but I can't. It's a wish that cannot be fulfilled. However, what you do have at your fingertips - what we all have, if only we can get in touch with it - is control over your own life.

> *You, and only you, are in the driving seat.*
> *You and only you are the one to run your life.*

It may feel quite often that it is not you, that it is the company you work for, the demands of your children, the rules of marriage, the unspoken 'oughts' of family life or the state that run your life. But actually, that is not the truth.

> *The truth is only you are in charge.*

Because of that, I would encourage you, right from the start of this book, to evoke the power of decision over your own life.

> *It's my life, I'm in charge, and I can decide what I want to do, with whom and when.*

Say the above, in front of a mirror, five times after brushing your teeth in the morning. Write it down and stick it on your fridge with a magnet. Whisper it on the way to work, put it in your phone, glue it to your computer or stick it on the cat's collar.

> *It's my life, I'm in charge, and I can decide what I want to do, with whom and when.*

Say it again in bed at night when you worry about the next day's workload and managing life's impossible demands.

Think it when your mother phones and guilt-trips you about not visiting, or your boss criticises your work and threatens cutting your hours back.

> *It's my life, I'm in charge, and I can decide what I want to do, with whom and when.*

This is a mantra against powerlessness and it reminds you, subconsciously, of who is in charge of your life. If you find it hard to say 'no' you will inevitably be feeling, somewhere deep down, that you are not in charge of things, that you have to please and appease others, that they come first and that you have no rights, no power of decision, over how you spend your time, energy and resources.

Well, you do.

Believe me, you do.

Believing you can't say 'no' is a habit, a pattern, an addiction, and like any of these it can be broken. Not easily, not overnight, but with time, effort, insight and support. You can do it.

Personally, although I have often found it hard to believe I'm in charge of my own life and I have had a difficulty about saying 'no', especially saying it effectively, *I'm definitely getting there.* Luckily, I have had the benefit of counselling, psychotherapy and life coaching not only to understand why it's difficult for me to say 'no', but also to learn new ways of being assertive and positive. As a consequence, this book — and you as a reader — will hopefully benefit from over twenty-five years of my own life experience. I have also worked with many people as a counsellor, trainer, life coach and psychotherapist on helping them evoke their own power of decision over their lives. I have also spoken to people who have responded to articles I have written about how hard, although necessary and possible, it is to say 'no', and they will pop up from time to time in this book.

Karen, a thirty-five-year-old primary teacher, emailed me in response to my article in *Woman* magazine about her inability to say 'no' to an overbearing father and his constant requests for her help. After our interview she emailed me: 'I really enjoyed talking to you and can see you must be a good therapist. I can also see what I've got to do now to deal with my dad. He's actually emotionally blackmailing me since my mum died and I've got to learn to stand up for myself and stop being a doormat. I can see how my dad guilt-trips me, just from our few exchanges, and I've got to give it up. After all, I've got my own life and the kids to think about.'

The right to your own life

Like many of us, Karen is struggling to embrace the right to have her life on her own terms. To do so, she will need to learn to accept - and love - who she is, warts and all. Each of us has to learn what our limits are, and understand we are doing our best, even when we feel we aren't. We can waste so much time and energy on wishing we were different, someone else, someone better. We worship the cult of perfection and celebrity ideals, and chastise ourselves for being ugly, fat, less than, stupid, badly flawed and hopeless wannabes. Yet, with a change of perspective, you could enjoy your life to the full. You could learn to say 'yes' to yourself and 'no' to impossible ideals and ridiculous role models. You could learn that you simply cannot earn love by running yourself ragged in the service of others, but you can learn to love yourself by accepting you are imperfect and tolerating yourself, just as you are.

Becoming your true self

If you find it hard to say 'no', you will probably find it hard to be your true self. It's quite easy to get stuck or paralysed by fear and anxiety; even so, perhaps you are ready to move forward decisively in your life? We are, after all, hopefully on a journey towards becoming our real, our true selves. Once you begin to grow up and become your true self, you can live life authentically, you can live your life to the full, and you are no longer pulled in too many directions at once.

To do that is to be fragmented, while to become your true self is to be an integrated whole. To this end, the other three parts of this book will focus on saying 'no' effectively, which will necessarily include you working out what it is you are actually doing with your life. The more on track you are, the easier it is to say 'no' to distracting, even tempting, things that come your way.

Time to think

As for me, I take time to think these days when the phone rings or someone asks me to do something for them, for others or for a good cause. 'Let me think about it' buys time to step back and work out whether I really want to do it, whether I can do it, whether I have the time and resources to commit to it, or whether I really just want a bit of a 'do-gooder' buzz to make myself feel better and to make them like me. (I'm conscious of my own Four 'Yes' Hooks.) As a consequence, I've gradually learned to say 'no' gracefully when I need to, and 'yes' when I can or want to. Effective 'no' saying is an art, and this book will offer you guidance on how to hone your skills. You *can* say 'no' and keep your friends and job. You *can* say 'no' and still be loved - you simply have to allow yourself full permission to live your own life on your terms:

> Does saying 'no' make you selfish, a bad person, lonely?
> Absolutely not.
> Will saying 'no' bring instant power and success?
> No, but it will bring you a sense of self.

Self-respect

Learning to say 'no' effectively brings you self-respect and therefore respect from those you want to respect you. It is also crucial for your children, if you have them, to see you saying 'no' effectively — how else can they learn to say 'no' themselves? For instance, it's important for your partner to respect your limits, and for your children to see you negotiating these boundaries successfully with each other. It's also important for colleagues to respect the fact that you have a life outside work that matters, and for friends to know you are not available 24/7. Also, elderly relatives need to understand that you will help them only within the limits of what you can really offer time- and energy-wise, because otherwise you can create havoc in your own relationship and family life and also disempower them by trying to do it all. Let's face it, a doormat is not a good role model and doesn't actually help anyone in the end.

However, being appropriately responsible and letting other people help themselves can bring you happier and healthier relationships and a more successful working and social life.

The Disease to Please

Finally, many women and men find it hard to say 'no' because they have got a bad dose of the 'Disease to Please', a phrase which Oprah Winfrey, the US talk show queen, coined on her TV show. The Disease to Please involves:

- saying 'yes' when you mean 'no';
- doing things for others without limits;
- putting other people first;
- not looking after your own needs.

So, are you a people-pleaser? Have you got the Disease to Please? Turn to the next chapter to find out.

2

Have you got the Disease to Please?

Being doorstepped

The doorbell rings. You're rushing to get out of the house for a special night out with friends; time is scarce and you're under pressure. Your pasta is boiling furiously on the stove and you have still to shower and get changed. You wonder whether to leave the door, but it could be something important. On the doorstep is a slick young man with a clipboard who smiles, flashes his ID and starts rattling off a sales pitch about a new telephone company. You find yourself pretending to listen, door ajar, with your mind on all you have to do to get out of the house on time. Each time you think he's about to pause, you take a breath to speak, but his sales pitch slides on to the next point, and the next. You begin to feel desperate - you want to shut him up *but you don't know how.* You try to butt into his well-oiled pitch and even consider slamming the door in his face, but every time you try he smiles sweetly and says, 'Yes, I can see you're busy, and I'll let you go, but just one more thing...' and off he goes again. Clearly he's been trained by Supertechno Sales Inc.: he's got to keep the patter going and he's got to close the deal. Anyway, part of you begins to get drawn into his sales pitch, almost against your will. It's only when you smell burning (oh no, my best pan!) and your mobile starts doing a wild fandango as your friends are making sure you're coming, that you're able to extricate yourself.

However, as you are closing the door the doorstepper moves closer, trying to pin you down: can he come back later? Tomorrow? Would you like a leaflet, a brochure, a cold call from his colleague? Do you have email? By now you are about to commit murder, scream, pull your hair out, shout fire, *anything* to get rid of him. When you eventually slam the door, loaded down with tariffs, brochures and phone, numbers, you find mayhem in the kitchen and it's too late to shower. In fact, you're late for everything...

Whose life is it anyway?

So why is it so hard to say, 'Stop, I don't have time for this', or, 'I don't buy things on the doorstep. Goodbye' (in frosty *Weakest Link* tones)? Of course, some people are very adept at closing the door on unwanted visitors - but this book is not for them. This book is for the thousands of us who find ourselves giving away our time, our energy, our money, our very selves, when, or perhaps *especially* when, we don't actually want to. The doorstepping scenario happens every day, in every way: political canvassers, religious fanatics or charity volunteers. It's easy to feel horribly trapped on your own doorstep or phone by someone trying to sell you something, or paying attention to someone when you don't want to. There you are, running along your own track, going about your business, then suddenly someone wants you to do something for them, to buy something or agree to their agenda. Or maybe they want you to listen to them: their problems, their sales pitch, even the gories about their stomach ulcer. You don't really want to be rude or thoughtless, but you also don't really want to be thrown off your own track. However, you can find yourself contorting into a double-back flip-flop loop-de-looper somersault trying to help, or listening until your ears drop off rather than being able to say a simple 'no' or extricate yourself from the situation.

Back to our doorstepper at the beginning of this chapter. What else could you do to handle the situation? Here's an action replay, with you acting decisively differently:

The doorbell rings. You're rushing to get out of the house for a special night out with friends: time is scarce and you're under pressure. Your pasta is boiling furiously on the stove and you still have to shower and get changed. You wonder whether to leave the door, but think it might be something important. On the doorstep is a slick young man with a clipboard who smiles, flashes his ID card and starts rattling off a sales pitch about a new telephone company. 'Sorry,' you say, looking him directly in the eye, 'but I haven't got time for this now.' He looks disgruntled, but continues charmingly, saying, 'Yes, I can see you're busy, and I'll let you go, but just one more thing ...' 'No,' you say, decisively, with a polite smile and looking him straight in the eye yet again, 'I have to go. Goodbye.' You close the door, with him protesting, 'Just take a leaflet...' Consequently, you eat your pasta, change and get out the house on time to have a great evening with your friends. When you come home, there's a sales brochure on the mat which you can read at leisure or simply put in the bin.

So what stops you acting decisively and confidently, as in the action replay above?

The reason?

You are probably a people-pleaser.

And...

You probably also find it hard to stand your ground with persuasive or bullying people.

And...

You don't like to offend or seem rude.

And...

You probably want to be liked. Very much.

People-pleasing

I'll admit it, I've been a terrible people-pleaser most of my life. Like a deranged good fairy, I get a kick out of being helpful, thoughtful and kind. I can find myself saying 'yes' before I think about the consequences. My arm shoots up, almost with a will of its own, volunteering me for all sorts of things I haven't got time for: organising the school fair, decorating friends' houses, helping heartbroken girlfriends, shopping for a sick neighbour, looking after someone's goldfish when they're away, or meeting an extra, impossible, deadline for work. Inevitably, I get a wonderful 'high' while performing these tasks, and I love the 'thank you' at the end (if there is one), but I usually overstretch myself and burn out, and end up feeling resentful after doing my good deeds. I also can end up feeling confused as to why I volunteered to help someone else out when my own life is full of unfinished business, half-done chores and unfulfilled dreams. I don't think I'm alone.

People-pleasing: top twenty traits

If you're a people-pleaser you'd rather pull your own teeth out manually than say 'no' to people, because:

1 you hate to let people down;
2 you feel responsible for everything and everyone;
3 you fear you may disappoint them if you don't do what they ask;
4 you feel, secretly, that other people just aren't as competent/capable/helpful as you are;
5 you get a kick out of being helpful;
6 being helpful gives your life meaning;
7 you double-guess people's needs before they ask;
8 you'd feel guilty if you didn't please others;
9 you find it easier to give than to receive;
10 it fills your time, gives you something to do;
11 you'd rather help someone out than help yourself;
12 you firmly believe people-pleasing makes the world go round;
13 you're a bit of a busybody, although you wouldn't like to admit it;
14 you have impossibly high standards which only you can meet;

15 you're addicted to helping others;
16 you feel good once you have been helpful (having earned your spiritual Brownie points);
17 it fits in with your religion, philosophy, value system, to put others before yourself;
18 you don't like to bother people with your problems;
19 you can't bear to hurt others and would rather hurt yourself;
20 you want to make everyone happy.

If any of the above rings true for you, you are probably a people-pleaser. The issue will be to work out the extent to which you are. This chapter is going to look, in more detail, at what people-pleasing actually is, where it comes from, and how it works. By the end of it, you should be able to identify more accurately whether you have the Disease to Please and what effect it may be having on your life.

The Disease to Please: symptoms

On the surface it would be easy to think the world would be a better place if we were all people-pleasers. Imagine it: people would stand up for the elderly or pregnant on buses and trains, children would never be bullied and nobody would have to cry alone, as others would rush to their defence or to put their arms around them. Indeed, as children most of us have been told to be 'nice' and 'polite' to people, especially strangers or the elderly. As grown ups, many of us strive to be good citizens and neighbours, model workers, firm friends, loyal lovers or family members.

Distinguish between being a helpful person and being a doormat

However, there is a need to distinguish between playing your part in your neighbourhood, at work, in relationships or in your family and being a chronic people-pleaser. It is important to understand the difference between being a helpful person and being an utter doormat. Of course, because each of us is unique, a list of symptoms may not cover your entire experience, but some things are generic to people-pleasers, as Min's story below illustrates.

People-pleasing patterns: Min's story

A thirty-one-year-old woman called Min emailed me from New Zealand, having read my article in *Woman* magazine about women finding it hard to say 'no'. I included myself in the article, as I had had many friendships with women during my twenties and thirties which always seemed to end up with a repeat pattern of being a 'doormat' best buddy (you know, side-kick to main star turn). I seemed to attract women friends who were always in crisis or having problems (boyfriend, money, work, sick cat, you name it). I would play best friend, mum and counsellor rolled into one, feeling very virtuous as I listened on the telephone for hours or cooked them supper or nursed them back to health. I always found myself saying things like 'Call me any time, night or day,' which I meant sincerely at the time. When they did, I'd feel pleased, at first, to be needed, and then unreasonably irritated and trapped by their ongoing level of need and demands.

Only problem was, once I needed something in return and asked for it (or, more often, hinted), I often didn't see them for dust. These friendships inevitably ended, usually badly. In response to my article, Min wrote feelingly: 'The subject of draining friends is one that's very pertinent to me at the moment. I have recently had a huge "blow out" with a girlfriend of fifteen years, which was very distressing. But I realise with hindsight that it was a one-sided friendship of the "fair weather" variety. What startled me was that I have ended up in the exact same situation again with an email penpal and I see a pattern forming.' Seeing a pattern forming is crucial. Once you begin to see that you repeat relationship patterns over and over, and that you may actually invite and even create them yourself, you can begin to do something about them. However, it can be uncomfortable, even painful, to see exactly what it is that you are doing. After all, it can be very comfortable to be operating on automatic, but once you acknowledge what is going on you can no longer (at least not easily) continue to kid yourself that it's fine really, or that you're simply a victim. Min continues, 'Why do I "need" these people in my life? I now realise I was getting a sense of "usefulness" out of these relationships, and while it's very satisfying on some levels it is not true friendship and I'm better off putting my efforts into something that is.' Ironically, Min writes at the bottom of her email, 'PS I wish you the best of luck with the book you are writing and hope to see it in print in NZ one day. It sounds like something I could well benefit from reading. Anything I can do to help?'

Happy Helper Habit

Those last six words give it all away. *'Anything I can do to help?'* It's probably just a knee-jerk response, but Min is writing to me about why she is always ending up in the same situation — being useful to everyone — and then is saying, almost in the same breath, 'Anything I can do to help?' The question here is: what would it be like for Min *not* to offer help? What would happen if she waited to be asked? Why, having told me she is beginning to be fed up with being useful, does she offer to be useful? Therein lies the rub - the symptoms of the Disease to Please necessarily involve what Tina, the hairdresser we met in Chapter 1, calls the Happy Helper Habit. Your mouth opens and offers help before your head has engaged. Similarly, Min is probably offering her help in the email to me before really having time to think, 'Do I really want to help? What would it involve? Or even, simply, have I got the time?'

Of course, we all say things like 'Can I help?', often in the happy expectation that this offer of help will not actually be taken up. This is part of the polite social fabric which weaves us together, rather like an automatic response we make to

'How are you?' 'Fine,' we reply, even if we are feeling down or hassled. The point here is, if you are a people-pleaser you may be saying 'Can I help?' not only far too often, on automatic pilot, but also in the hope that your offer of help will be taken up, *regardless* of whether you really, truly want to help, or even have the time or resources to dedicate to doing that.

People-pleasing isn't pleasing

So what makes a perfectly intelligent person offer help when they don't really mean it, or don't really want to? I have been in this situation so many times myself, it feels horribly familiar. People-pleasing isn't about pleasing people: it's actually about *controlling others*. By making others dependent on you, you actually bind them to you. It can actually be a way of trying to make yourself central to someone else's life and, in that sense, is quite narcissistic. Thus, chronic people-pleasing is a way of making others beholden to you. It can feel very uncomfortable to be on the receiving end of this kind of pattern of behaviour, because, suddenly, you're in emotional debt at the Happy Helper Bank and have to pay it all back, often with interest.

People-pleasing can also be about interfering in other people's lives by being intrusive and trying to live vicariously through them. Some people do this because they feel their own lives are meaningless, or they have underachieved. Sometimes it is to make themselves feel important or essential, because in fact they have low self-esteem and self-worth. If you have the Disease to Please you want other people to see you in a certain way: you want them to think, 'Oh, so-and-so is such a wonderful, fantastic person, they did this for me,' or 'So-and-so is so clever, they were able to do that, when no one else could.' There is a link here with having a 'saviour complex', which means you may have the need to be a martyr, a hero, someone who performs superhuman feats with no qualms about the cost to self. Of course, this is really a fantasy rather than a reality, because repressing your own needs for the sake of others is the stuff of films and novels, but in real life, in real relationships, it works somewhat differently. We all have needs and we all need them to be met, and to this end people-pleasing can actually be a form of psychic manipulation, whose aim is to control others.

Nice isn't really nice

The thing about being nice all the time is that it's not real. Nobody can be nice all the time: we all have parts of us which are bad-tempered, irritable, greedy, critical, and thinking you are a 100 per cent nice person is a way of trying to bolster your low self-esteem and self-confidence. There are two main problems about thinking you are completely nice. First, it's a defence against being criticised ('How can he say that about me, when I'm so nice?') which actually leaves you quite open to criticism. If you think you are wholly nice and someone has had a go at you, you feel attacked and wounded. We call people 'brittle' when they are like this. They bristle at any hint of criticism and take everything very seriously. The slightest comment or even a look drives them into a frenzy of uncertainty. You can hear women talking about their women friends, saying, 'I don't know why so-and-so doesn't like me — after all, I've been so *nice* to her.' That's actually the problem. We think being nice will somehow protect us against unfair comment, or will, actually buy us friendship. Usually it has the opposite effect. People feel uncomfortable with people who are always so damned good, who smile a lot and never grouch about anything. It feels phoney to them, and in fact *it is phoney*. We all have our dark sides and to pretend otherwise is to deny the totality of yourself. Nobody is a total Pollyanna. Everyone has good bits and bad bits, dark vices and light virtues. You can't really have sun without shadow, as a picture which was all bright sunshine would have no contrast, perspective or depth.

However, believing you are nothing but nice (like a stick of rock with 'nice' printed all the way through it) is a psychological defence which was built to protect you when you were very young and felt unable to protect yourself. So if this is true of you, don't come down on yourself like a sledgehammer. Rather, try and understand more about why you need to be seen to be a perfect goody-two-shoes all the time.

Too nice for my own good: Hannah's story

Hannah, twenty-six, who works as a nanny, goes out of her way to be 'nice' to everyone. 'I've spent my life desperate to be liked and this ends up with me apologizing all the time for everything, or making things "nice" for everyone. I would always make sure everyone had a cup of tea, or was sitting comfortably or felt OK.' Although these are perfectly honourable behaviours, Hannah in fact drives her friends mad. 'They say to me, "For goodness sake, stop fussing about," or "Sit down and drink your own tea, you're making me feel uncomfortable."' Hannah was brought up very strictly: 'I was taught children were seen and not heard and that you shouldn't ever ask for anything because you wouldn't get it.' She knows now that she became a nanny because 'I wanted to give to children what I wanted for myself,' so she has made everything extra nice for children, hoping she will someday reap the benefit vicariously. A modern-day Mary Poppins, Hannah has begun to understand that it is impossible to be nice all the time to everyone. 'When I turned twenty-five I thought, "I'm not very satisfied with my life, and making it nice for everyone else is getting me nowhere" - I'm now fearful of staying in the same place and if I continue putting the focus on helping others I'll never, ever help myself.'

Magical thinking

People-pleasers, like Hannah, are full of what psychologists call 'magical thinking'. This stems from childhood, when you think if you close your eyes and wish hard enough your wildest dream will come true. If you want it hard enough you can actually make it happen, is how it goes. It can go hand in hand with a belief that you are totally omnipotent - that is, all powerful. In this state you believe that, given a superhuman effort, you can and will achieve anything and everything. There is a fantasy that if you work hard enough, try hard enough, are good enough, nice enough, then all will work out perfectly. As in people-pleasing, magical thinking is really about trying to control your environment and not being able to face reality. This kind of thinking is fine in childhood as, after all, children grow and learn through fantasising. But if this persists into adulthood, you may find yourself in trouble emotionally. 'Magical thinking' is actually a psychological defence against feeling small, vulnerable and powerless. However, being power-drunk promotes a feeling of false power, a feeling that you actually have a magic wand, worthy of Harry Potter or any typical good fairy, and you can make things happen. The focus of your magic and power dreams is managing other people's lives. You begin to fantasise that you are, in fact, the good fairy in the fairytales and you can make things come true for others. This can fill you up with a wonderful feeling of power and goodness, especially if you are feeling particularly powerless and bad about yourself and your own life at the time.

Blanket rules

The thing about people-pleasers is that you can make blanket rules about things: always be nice to people, put others first, don't be rude, etc. The truth is, in the same way as you need to distinguish between being a helpful person and being a doormat, you also need to make distinctions between types of people. If you behave nicely to everyone, regardless of how they behave towards you, you will come unstuck. A blanket rule to make everyone like you is guaranteed to fail. Do you really want everyone to like you, including people you don't actually like or respect or admire? Surely not. Would you work hard to please someone who is really quite rude, selfish, thankless, aggressive or nasty? If so, then you place yourself in a very vulnerable position because you have not learned to assess people and see their differences, or to protect yourself emotionally.

Boundaryless

The problem is, too, that if you try to be nice and please everyone, regardless of how they treat you, you are boundaryless. We all need firm psychological and physical boundaries to keep ourselves safe and sane. You need to understand clearly where you begin and the other person ends. Not having an emotional boundary, even with your nearest and dearest, leaves you open to overuse and abuse. The doormat mentality means you are only there to have muddy feet wiped upon you. This is clearly not a position of self-respect or self-confidence, but, indeed, the humiliating place of the lowest of the low. You will need to identify your boundaries and firm them up if you are going to learn to say no, and to say it effectively.

Disease to Please checklist

Having read thus far, perhaps you are still wondering if you have the Disease to Please. Take a moment to read the following checklist of key symptoms. Be as honest as you can with yourself as you read. Do you:

1 feel wonderful, almost 'high', when you please people, and afterwards often feel resentful, irritated, critical, annoyed, even used?
2 do things for others out of a sense of duty or obligation?
3 feel you 'ought' or 'should' do things for people?
4 sometimes feel you live a 'Jekyll and Hyde' existence: presenting a 'nice' face to the world, a 'nasty' face to those closest to you?

5 get preoccupied with other people's problems and worry about them a lot, puzzling out how you could be helpful to them?

6 attract friends who are 'prima donnas' and/or 'the walking wounded?'

7 convince yourself that other people's needs come first, that others are worse off than you, that you are pretty lucky in life and need nothing and no one really?

8 feel over-responsible for everything and everyone? Thank goodness you're around, otherwise nothing would ever get done; thank heavens you were there when something happened, otherwise, who knows, disaster may have struck...

9 feel very critical of people who are incapable? You almost hold them in contempt, but you would never, ever, show it, especially to them.

10 make friendships and relationships which seem to repeat patterns - you're always the strong one, the others are users or useless, or you feel used and the other takes too much? You get disappointed in people fairly quickly, as a consequence.

11 become very enthusiastic about a new relationship or friendship, but then it all seems to go horribly wrong and, surprise, surprise, it ends up like the last time, even though it looked so different and promising at first?

12 feel very lonely and isolated deep down, but find it hard to admit? So you fill your time with useful, helpful activity.

13 let people's needs dominate your life: your family, your children, your husband, your friends, your colleagues and casual acquaintances (people down at the gym, your neighbours, etc.)? Do they all seem more important than you?

14 never seem to get the things on your own personal agenda done? You've wanted to change jobs, get married, get divorced, move house, start a business, or learn a new skill for years, but you haven't got round to it yet, because you haven't got the time...

15 find it hard to be honest about your feelings or straight in your dealings because you want absolutely everyone to like you — so you simply can't offend anyone?
16 always seem to spend more when you go out with friends or a partner - you drive them home, or listen more than they do, or host meals, or organise things, or bail them out financially, and you wonder why; and although you seem to do it all, actually, deep down you think it's really unfair?

How did you score?

If you have 0—5 'yes' answers to the above, you need to watch out for your people-pleasing tendencies, but are doing quite well in setting boundaries.

If you have 5—10 'yes' answers, you jump in a bit too fast, perhaps are overly concerned with other people's problems and try to please others too much. Take time to think about your own needs and how to meet them for yourself.

Between 11 and 16 'yes' answers? Oh dear. You are definitely a chronic people-pleaser, and I'm afraid your confidence is probably quite low. Pleasing people is a way of life and you probably feel very awkward indeed about having or doing anything for yourself. Keep reading this book.

It will be useful at this point to note down in your notebook or on your computer file how much of a people-pleaser you think you are. As you read the book you may find yourself having fresh insights, rethinking your behaviour and making decisions. Note these down. It is easy to 'forget' what you have understood as your psychological patterns take over again and push you back into operating on automatic. If you want to change how you behave, you will first have to acknowledge and accept what you actually do. Hopefully, by the end of this book you will be in more of a position of *choosing* what you do, rather than being a people-pleasing robot, fuelled by guilt and unworthiness. Hopefully, too, you will be systematically building your self-esteem and confidence and putting yourself at the centre of your own life (see Chapter 10: Living free of the Disease to Please).

Addictive behaviour

Finally, when the Disease to Please rules your life it can be an addictive behaviour. This means you feel you can't do anything but behave as you do, but you are often, deep down, really quite unhappy about how your life is going. Underlying all of our everyday emotional addictions there are usually painful feelings which we try to keep at bay. These feelings stem from our childhood experiences, and before you can begin to say 'no' effectively in your life it is important to understand a bit more about what might be making saying 'no' feel impossible. To this end, we will now turn to the deeper, but quite common, psychological reason for avoiding saying 'no': the addiction to helping others.

3

Are you addicted to helping?

The phone rings; it's late at night and you're just getting into bed, exhausted and ready to snuggle down with a good book before falling asleep. On the phone is your distraught friend, whose boyfriend has left her *yet again* (she's always having crises). You want to go to sleep but you also want to help, although you feel a bit wary about the same old drama happening again. So you button your lip and listen for about an hour while she wails in your ear. You *do* feel sorry for her, after all, because she never seems to pick the right man. While listening you find yourself feeling drawn into the drama, and get a buzz from feeling indispensable. Thank goodness you were there to help — who knows what would have happened if you had ignored the call or had simply read your book? However, when you put the phone down you feel wide awake and grumpy, you sleep badly and are late for work the next day.

What else could you have done? If you'd interrupted your deeply distressed friend right at the beginning by saying, 'Listen, I'm so sorry, but I'm really tired ...' what would have happened? Would she have hung up and not talked to you for a week - or, perhaps, forever? Or maybe she would have thought you were 'selfish' and not like the old you anymore? Were you even frightened she would lose it and commit suicide? Perhaps it would have been extremely awkward and you would have been drenched in guilt to have snuggled down to enjoy your book rather than listen to her tale of woe? Or could it be that you got drawn into her drama, despite yourself, not only relishing the gory details but also getting a bit of an ego boost out of being her late-night saviour? Anyway, you've probably convinced yourself that you're 'best friends', and surely 'best friends' should be there for each other, night and day, no matter what? So you really did the right thing, didn't you?

Did you?

Well, no, not really.

Listening to someone when you don't want to doesn't actually help them. If you feel resentful, half asleep, irritated and obliged, you are not really going to listen well or with an open heart. What's more, making yourself tired and late for work doesn't help anyone either.

It's a dilemma. Particularly because you can fall into this kind of a pattern with a friend, which can damage the relationship long term. So what can you do?

Let's try an action replay of the above late-night scenario and see if there could be a different outcome.

The phone rings. It's late at night and you're just getting into bed, exhausted and ready to snuggle down with a good book before falling asleep. On the phone is your distraught friend, whose boyfriend has left her *yet again* (she's always having crises). You want to go to sleep but you want to help, so you say, 'I'm really sorry to hear your news, and it shouldn't be happening to you, as you're such a lovely person. Listen, I can't listen long now as I'm in bed and I've got work in the morning, but I do care, so could we meet for lunch of maybe a drink after work this week?' She might protest, or even cry for five more minutes, but you might well put the phone down with a meeting arranged at a time that doesn't exhaust you or ruin your work day. If you can do this, you will have conveyed that you care - which you do — and when you meet it's more likely that you'll be in the right frame of mind to listen constructively and be genuinely supportive.

More importantly, you will have shifted the responsibility back on to your friend to look after herself. Before you hang up the phone, you could even give her a few minutes to think who else she could call late at night, as there will probably be at least one other person available.

Going back to the action replay - what do you think about it? Are you shocked and outraged at the selfishness of turning down a friend in need? Does it seem a cheek to send them to someone else? Or is it a relief to think you could act that way? Do you fear you'd lose this friend for good if you did behave this way? Well, if you did fall out, you'd have to examine what the friendship was really about. A good friend would think about you before phoning late at night (is it convenient for you because you have children or have to work in the morning?) and also they would probably understand if you said you couldn't listen right then, but later. They might not like it, but in a mutually supportive friendship these things have to be negotiated. The friend who makes you feel you are over an emotional barrel is not a friend: they are a drain. If you feel you can't say 'no' to them, then your life is actually running down that drain.

Addiction to helping

There was a time in my own life when I was at the beck and call of anyone in trouble, as in the scenario above. I was running a large counselling network, with responsibility for training counsellors and teachers as well as teaching myself. It was a big, largely unpaid, responsibility that I did outside full-time work. Over a decade my counselling activities began to take over my life in all sorts of ways. Every day I had letters and phone calls from people who needed me in some way, and I would write or call them back and give them my time, my help and myself. (My phone bills were huge.) It felt great. It was like a drug. I was important, I could help someone, and I was essential. I was also a great source of (often unsolicited) advice. I was always thinking about other people, always putting myself out for one cause or another. My day job was also 'caring', as I worked for a civil rights organisation. During this time I was involved in launching a couple of national campaigns which involved hard, unpaid graft. Naturally, I volunteered to be shop steward, and then convenor, for my workplace union - so the welfare of my colleagues was also in my hands. I also taught evening classes, which took time and effort to prepare and run. What a superwoman, on the go all the time! People used to say, 'I don't know how you do it all,' and I felt very gratified. I definitely needed to be needed. I put myself out for people whenever I could. My life wasn't measured out in coffee spoons, as in T.S. Eliot's poem 'The Love Song of J. Alfred Prufrock', it was measured out in the number of poor souls I had saved or was actively saving on all fronts all the time. I loved seeing my students flourish, I felt fulfilled when my counselling clients bloomed, I felt like a saviour when I was there when road crashes or heart attacks happened (of course, I'd done first aid). I was a superduper coper, a helper, a rescuer, simply a vitally important person to have around.

Not.

Oh boy, was I addicted to helping.

Oh dear, had I got a large dose of grandiosity.

Nobody is that indispensable. Not even the Prime Minister or the Pope. It can just be a comforting illusion to think you are.

What happened? I got ill a lot. First of all migraines, then flulike symptoms and stomach aches. Every few weeks I would disappear from my onerous, but terribly important, duties and take to my bed, feeling achey and feverish. I wanted some looking after, I needed some nourishing, but I would usually have to do it for myself (I found it hard to take, back then). Soon I would surface and recover, only to willingly take on my harness of over-responsibility and compulsive caring again. I began to think something was really wrong when, after a relaxing holiday in the sun, I came home to about a hundred letters and about fifty phone messages. As I opened my letters and listened to my messages something happened: I ceased to feel relaxed and free after my holiday abroad, and instead a dark cloud came over me and I got a migraine and felt sick. I suddenly had the experience of putting my head inside something very tight and dark. I felt stifled. Then I began to feel resentful, even angry, about why I was doing all this, largely for free. There seemed to be a psychological noose around my neck. Why was I putting my own neck in there voluntarily? What on earth was I getting out of it all? Why was I carrying the world on my shoulders? I was hooked on helping and it was ruining my life.

At the time I was wanting to have a baby and write novels, but, of course, I didn't have the time. Many of my friendships had to be put on hold because I was always too busy to go out to play. At work, I was not doing what I really wanted to do because I was too busy sorting everybody else's lives out. As for love - well, I made sure I couldn't spend all that much time on a relationship because I was always needed elsewhere. Needless to say, my love life wasn't very intimate and satisfying back then and relationships tended to come and go.

Compulsive Carers Corp.

I have discovered over the years that many people drawn to the caring professions are, in fact, themselves compulsive carers, like I used to be. Nurses, doctors, surgeons, counsellors, teachers, aid workers, health visitors, nuns and priests, vicars and their wives/husbands, charity workers, therapists, trainers, psychologists, campaigners, hospice staff, union workers, housewives/househusbands, foster parents, volunteers and 'nice', 'caring' people of all colours, shapes and sizes: they often have a life membership to Compulsive Carers Corp., of which I was a definite founder member.

Veronica's story: a compulsive carer's secret life

I used to run Overcoming Addictions workshops for the counselling network I was involved in (for more on this, see my book *Overcoming Addiction: Positive Steps for Breaking Free of Addiction and Building Self-Esteem*, e-book available on Amazon). These were weekend or day events, where people had a chance to own up to their everyday chemical and emotional addictions in a safe environment and get a chance to look at the underlying emotions which kept the addictions in place. One weekend I met a wonderful woman I will call Veronica. She was nearly sixty but looked more like forty. She was slender, with smooth skin and bright shining eyes, and very charming: Veronica was a successful yoga teacher, who ran workshops and classes herself. Indeed, she was so successful she was beginning to be stressed out by her level of success and the demand on her emotional resources and time. After the first workshop group, where we all owned up to our addictions (to cheers of encouragement and lots of laughter), Veronica spoke out. She owned up, with tears of shame and giggles of embarrassment: 'I work as a yoga teacher,' she explained, 'but I come home after a class or workshop and down at least two double whiskies.' Instead of gasps of incredulity or disapproval, the group kept listening. 'I just get so drained and overwhelmed by giving out all the time to other people, I find I have no time to do my yoga properly for myself,' she admitted, 'so I'm downing whiskies so I can relax quickly and get some sleep.' The irony of her situation was not lost on the group, and not least Veronica herself. 'How could I have got myself into this position?' she asked us all, but herself in particular. 'I think of myself as a healer, and I'm trying to help others all the time to heal themselves, but the effort of doing so is making me harm myself instead.' The old adage, 'Healer, heal thyself', springs to mind. Interestingly, Veronica told us she came from a poor, working-class background, where she had seen her mother nearly kill herself doing menial factory work and bringing up three children, while her father was a casual labourer, often unemployed. Veronica felt deeply guilty that, through education (she'd passed the old eleven-plus exam), she had moved out of the working class and up the class ladder into comfortable middle-classdom. However, her guilt at now being cosy and privileged had left her drowning in self-reproach. Even living her alternative lifestyle, she still felt bad that she had it so good, so she was giving out more and more and emptying out her own resources. 'I can't ever forget the picture of my mother working her fingers to the bone for us,' she said, 'and we had to pull our weight as kids, too. I guess I felt I ought to save others and that somehow that would save my mum - although it's too late now, as she's dead.' Veronica explained she gets a great high from helping people, but at the back of her mind she is also scared she'll end up like her mum, burnt out, even dead before her time. She felt very ashamed about drinking whisky as a holistic healer and felt she would be 'found out' as a sham before long.

Codependency

The most important part of this story, in a way, is the fact that Veronica was able to own up to the seeming contradictions in her life. Looked at in terms of her childhood, it would seem logical that she would need to fill up where she felt empty, in order to give limitlessly to others. And that also, as a carer, her nurturing of others was, in fact, a way of trying to nurture herself.

Now it's important to get something clear here. Of course we need people who care. The world could not go round at all well without having people who care for others. We obviously need people like Veronica to make things go well. Without these kinds of people, things would not change, people would not be helped and life would be far more miserable for millions. However, we know these kinds of jobs are often undervalued and the people overused in our culture because they are seen to have a 'vocation' or a 'calling'. Because of that, we often expect the people drawn to these professions to give their very lifeblood. They work long hours, often for very little or low pay. They go the extra mile and put themselves at risk, often on a regular basis, and they also burn out frequently. Our society depends on their dedication and hard work.

However, the very thing that drives people to do this kind of work can also drive them to accept poor conditions and to put their own needs last. The psychological need that being a compulsive carer tries to meet can also lead them to give too much of themselves in a boundaryless way. The root of this kind of problem has been identified for some time now and is called codependency. Codependents belong to Compulsive Carers Corp. They only feel happy when they are caring for others. They will deny their own needs and put others first. In *Codependency: How to Break Free and Live Your Own Life* (Piatkus) the authors, Liz Hodgkinson and the late David Stafford, aptly describe codependency as being 'a way of getting your needs met that doesn't get your needs met'.

As we have seen above, the caring professions are crawling with codependents, people who will serve others with no thought of their own welfare, until, of course, they burn out, their relationships fall apart, they get ill and/or addicted, even die. This may sound extreme, but codependency can drain you of all your resources to the point that you may have to break down to break free.

Back in the 1960s in America, Alcoholics Anonymous did some groundbreaking research about alcoholic families. They found that when the - back then, usually male - alcoholic in a family gave up the booze and dried out, something strange happened. His marriage or relationship would collapse. This was an odd outcome, because up until then his usually long-suffering wife or partner would have been saying, 'If only he'd stop drinking, we'd be happy.' The research revealed that codependents - the wives or partners of alcoholics - actually needed their husband or partner to keep drinking to keep the relationship afloat. Why? The person living with the alcoholic needs the drinker to need them. Co-dependents wrap themselves around their alcoholic partners, propping them up, talking about them endlessly to friends, putting up with their bad behaviour by being a doormat. For, without their partners being hopeless alcoholics, they have no role in life. Indeed, it was found that codependents actually encouraged and sustained their partners' drinking, albeit unconsciously, because if they dried out, what would they, the codependents, do with their lives?

Think about it.

If you find yourself caring or helping compulsively, is there any way in which you are inadvertently keeping the other person or people dependent on you to give your own life meaning? Or perhaps you are deflecting attention away from your own problems? If you always end up mopping up the sick after your partner has drunk too much, are you colluding with their drinking? If you are the one in your extended family who always looks after your parents when they are ill or jumps in when something needs doing, are you gaining something from this, even though you moan about it and feel hard done by or exhausted sometimes? If you are a mother, do you make yourself the hub of your family by doing everything for everyone? Do you try to bind people to you by becoming indispensable in their lives? What is the emotional payback of being a saint and dogsbody rolled into one?

Codependents actually need to control other people by tying them to them through being important and essential. You make others feel that you will be there for them, no matter what. You worry about them all the time, perhaps phoning them to check they are all right, or leaving little thoughtful notes for them. Maybe you remember their appointments for them or think about ways of solving their problems for them? Perhaps you lend them money, give them clothes, cook their food, do their work for them or even handle authority or difficult people on their behalf? The problem with all this is that you keep the other person in a child-like mode, just so that you can feel big and needed and grown up.

What has codependency got to do with saying 'no'?

Well, if you are codependent, you will find it almost impossible to say 'no'. You will be so hooked on being useful to give meaning to your life that you will lay yourself at the feet of the person who needs you, while telling yourself that, indeed, it is the other who is the needy one. You are a veritable doormat, although you actually manipulate the other person's feet to wipe themselves on you. In fact, codependents are extremely needy people, *but they deny their own needs.* They actually give to others what they need for themselves. By denying their own needs - for love, respect, kindness, care, help - they retain a feeling of being in charge. If they were to own up to feeling needy, they would feel powerless and out of control, which would be very threatening and scary indeed. Often the codependent despises need and, to some extent, they hold the needy person who drains them in contempt (hence they feel resentful when helping them, although this may remain an unconscious feeling). Thus, by making other people the problem they can retain a feeling of omnipotence and deny any uncomfortable feelings of vulnerability or need.

Codependents often work until they drop; they don't know they are tired, ill, emotionally empty, hungry or thirsty, as they don't really care about themselves. Often immaculately turned out (they want to be perfect), they will nonetheless put all their attention on the other person in the hope that they will, eventually, be thanked or loved for helping. In fact, this seldom happens, because even if the person on the receiving end of the compulsive caring says 'thanks' or even loves their helper, the codependent will be quick to push them away and deny their love, not believing they have made any difference, and not being able to take in the very praise that they actually crave.

The roots of codependency

This may sound very perverse and complicated, but it is far more commonplace than we realise in our society, largely because so many people feel unloved and have such low self-confidence and self-esteem. The roots of codependency lie in our families of origin and in our childhood experiences. For instance, if you come from a family where one or more parents or carers:

- drink alcohol or do drugs to excess,
- are workaholic,
- are severely mentally or physically disabled,
- are codependent themselves,
- are unhappy and the family doesn't work very well as a family ('dysfunctional'),
- abuse their power by being violent, sexually or physically abusive, or all three,
- are emotionally distant, unexpressive or constantly critical and negative,
- are 'emotionally illiterate': that is, unable to understand feelings,

then you may well have developed codependent tendencies in reaction to not feeling loved, safe, cared for or valued. Does any of the above ring true for you? Can you identify characteristics of your parents in the above list? Take time out to write down what you remember about your mother and father (or carers) in terms of their own behaviour and characteristics. Did you feel loved, safe and cared for? Was it enough? What did your family make you feel like and what sort of role did you adopt, as a consequence? Note these thoughts down in your notebook or on your computer file, for future reference.

'I became a little mother': Rose's story

Rose is a fifty-eight-year-old Irish nurse with three grown-up sons who is a self-confessed codependent. I advertised for people to talk to me for this book through the National Association for Children of Adult Alcoholics (NACOA) network. NACOA do a great deal of work helping codependents recover from their compulsive caring addiction, particularly through self-help groups. Amazingly, Rose, who had spent most of her life in an abusive relationship with a man who was always having affairs, has finally freed herself from the grip of the relationship through reading self-help books, like this one, five years ago. She is still single and incredibly happy today. 'My father was a binge drinker, a dypsomaniac,' explains Rose, 'and I was the eldest of four. As the eldest girl I had to be able to step into my mother's shoes at any time to run the family. My mother found it hard to cope with my father's drinking and he was violent towards her, which was terrifying.'

Rose learned to look after her three younger siblings, and her mother as well, who was often emotionally or physically overwhelmed. At the same time, Rose went to the Roman Catholic church, which taught her the virtues of self-sacrifice and self-denial. Rose often found herself wedged between her parents, trying to calm her father down and soothe her mother. 'I became a little mother myself and I learned to pacify difficult situations. I didn't think about myself at the time because I was busy looking after everyone else. I was so responsible, for everything and everyone.' This is a hallmark of codependency, children being made to feel responsible and old before their time. 'My mother fed this back to me daily: "Oh, I don't know what I would do without her, she's so good," which made me feel wanted, I suppose.'

However, Rose was unprepared by her family experiences for real adult life. She discovered, once she'd left home and had gone overseas to England to train as a nurse, that her compulsive caring patterns made her vulnerable to abuse. 'I made a huge number of mistakes, as emotionally I was very much a child. I fell into sexual relationships too easily because I was desperate for affection and was easily flattered and seduced. I also liked to be helpful. I was always doing favours for friends and running ragged, doing things for other people.' And, of course, her career choice of being a nurse fitted perfectly with her codependency.

But deep inside, underneath her Happy Helper mask, Rose was really miserable, lonely and afraid. 'I had no self-confidence and less self-esteem, and I felt utterly unlovable, so I let my partner get away with murder.' She had one of those rollercoaster relationships which was constantly on and off, with her man treating her badly and philandering, which would make Rose throw him out, then relent and take him back. Why did she take back someone who didn't respect her at all? 'There was a well of love inside of me that I wanted to give,' explains Rose, 'which made me put up with being treated badly. He convinced me I had no right to expect any more from him, and I fell for it because I didn't feel I had any right to be loved for myself.' So how did she change the situation? Reading a self-help book by Claudia Black, called *It Will Never Happen to Me* (Random House, 1987), was the turning-point for Rose. 'I was aghast, as I could see myself on every page. It blew my mind and I gradually became more assertive, which meant we fought more.' Now Rose demanded more from her partner and her relationship, so he was confronted by her more. It made their relationship and life together very uncomfortable, and they argued as she fought for her self-respect.

Then he 'tested' her resolve, with yet another affair, and for the first time in twenty years Rose issued an ultimatum which she really meant. He was amazed and simply didn't believe her, but for the first time in her life Rose truly meant it. With counselling support, Rose was able to resist taking her partner back once his affair was over. 'I said no. I said no to accepting the relationship on his terms, I said no to his coming back, I said no to his having my hard-earned money, I said no to everything he wanted me to do. He was astonished. It was very hard for me to do, but it was also utterly wonderful. I threw him out for good. I still loved him, but I wanted to have my life back. I had to do this to get some self-esteem, and the most important thing was, I had to learn to be myself.'

I tell Rose's story at length here because it really is a classic example of codependency. Her alcoholic father, her weak, un-protective mother, her role as 'little mother' to all the family, set her up for life as a compulsive carer. As a supposed grown up, she was not able to take care of herself as she had no real emotional or physical boundaries. Rose gave to others what she needed for herself: love, care, money, time, respect and power. 'When you begin to recover you start seeing things for what they really are,' explains Rose, 'and when you do that you can't really go back. Before that I felt at the mercy of the wind.'

Golden rules of giving up compulsive caring

If the above story rings any bells for you, it might make you think about why or how you have become a compulsive carer. Think back to your own childhood: what can you see that made you over-responsible, feel unloved, and old before your time? Did you feel love was conditional, that it had to be 'earned' if you were very good? Were you frightened into thinking self-sacrifice was the right way to get affection? Whatever, it's a good idea to write down, if you can, your own early life story. Read it through carefully and look for clues about yourself and your behaviour. If you feel you can't say 'no' to people because you have no right or they scare you, or you simply appease and please all the time, try and trace back your problems to their roots, like Rose above, through telling your own childhood story. Meanwhile, there are some golden rules about giving up compulsive caring. You need to:

- believe other people - not you - are responsible for their own lives, and give them back that responsibility;
- put attention on your own problems and get all the help you need to solve them, including seeing a counsellor or therapist;
- catch yourself when you want to help — and bite your tongue, sit on your hands, wait and see if someone else takes charge instead of you;
- care appropriately for your own children — they really need you to give them unconditional love and care with firm boundaries;
- make your own life number one on your 'to do' list;
- don't pick up 'hints' to help others - let them go;

- be aware that you are trying to make yourself feel worthwhile and loved by compulsive caring - learn to love yourself for who you are, warts and all, instead;
- make a list of your ten best attributes and stick them on the fridge - and recite them daily;
- challenge or drop people who simply use, or even abuse, you one-way;
- make friends and relationships which are mutually caring and loving (and notice when or if they reciprocate);
- learn to take gracefully;
- ask for what you want (don't expect your mind to be read);
- learn to say 'no', without a preamble or justifications;

and, most important of all:

- put yourself first.

Changing codependent patterns

Change does not occur overnight, change is gradual. 'Change comes about by being truly yourself instead of trying to be something else,' explains Gestalt Therapist, Nu Tran. 'If you try to be something you're not you'll never be yourself, but when you are yourself, change will naturally come about. That's the paradoxical theory of change.' Nu Tran explains this Gestalt theory further: 'If you know yourself, then you can accept yourself and know what you want, and change can occur.' As Rose demonstrated, once you acquire self-knowledge and self-awareness (and once you can allow yourself to get the emotional nourishment you need) there is no going back. As for me, one counselling teacher I had noticed my compulsive caring tendencies were draining me dry and he gave me a useful direction to follow. He suggested that from now on I 'step over my loved ones' bleeding bodies'. It was a metaphorical direction, of course. What he meant was that I adopt an attitude and posture of putting myself first and waiting to see if someone else stepped in to do the rescuing. On a psychological level, he was suggesting that I stop seeing all the suffering everywhere in the world as my sole responsibility (what classic omnipotence!) and, instead, get on with my own life constructively. Since then I've noticed that, say, if I'm on the street and someone is in trouble or falls over or is ill, there is usually at least one other person who will step in to help. It doesn't always have to be me who rushes in, and indeed, if I hang back for thirty seconds watching the situation, I have noticed others will usually step in. That doesn't mean to say I would let someone be seriously hurt or die - of course I wouldn't. It does mean, however, that I have learned that I am not the only one around who can help. I don't have to be the superhero of my own life (or other people's) to give my life meaning or to feel good. The cost to my life and my health was far too great when I was compulsively caring for everything that breathed. I now can choose where I put my energies because I can see that my resources are limited and I am, after all, only human. What's more, I've finally given other people around me back their responsibility for their own lives. Of course, this kind of process will bring up feelings, and it is to this issue - facing the feelings that stop you saying no - that we now turn.

4

Facing the feelings that make it hard to say 'no'

How do you feel when you say 'no'? Is it easy peasy, simple as can be? OK as long as you feel comfortable with someone? Or do you feel guilty, awkward and embarrassed and simply can't get the word 'no' out? Of course, there will be many different situations in which you need to say 'no' - and there are, therefore, many different ways of saying 'no'. If someone asks you if you'd like coffee (and you hate it) you can say a simple 'no, thanks'. But what if you feel shy, and perhaps you are in a situation where you don't know the person very well or you want to impress? You might well say 'yes' just to keep things simple and sweet (and then leave your coffee to get cold). However, if someone comes up to you on the street and tries to take your bag, you may well bellow 'no' at the top of your voice, even if you think you are shy and passive. We face myriad situations every day which require us to make negative decisions and voice them. However, it is probably fair to say that if you feel saying 'no' is hard, even impossible, it may well be that your *feelings* are getting in the way. This chapter will examine what those feelings might be — and how to identify them — in order to help you learn to say 'no' more effectively.

What are feelings for?

We have feelings for a purpose: they motivate us to act in all sorts of ways, so it is important to 'tune in' to your feelings in order to learn how you feel and what you do or do not want. The main feelings that stop us saying 'no' are probably quite negative or uncomfortable ones: fear, anxiety, guilt, anger, embarrassment and self-consciousness. These sorts of feelings usually indicate a dislike or a discomfort, but if you can let yourself feel them, they can motivate you to say 'no'. Feelings are emotions and emotions occur naturally within us to help us live our lives successfully (and, of course, to stay alive). In order to tune in with your emotions, you need to ask yourself, 'What am I feeling?' I once did a wonderful course called 'The Mastery' at the Actors' Institute in London. We spent the whole weekend with the tutor pausing every so often and asking us, 'What are you feeling?' We learned to tune in to how we felt and to articulate those feelings, and it was a totally fascinating and liberating experience to do so. I felt more in charge of myself as a consequence. If you can recognise your feelings, you can also learn what they are trying to tell you. For instance, if you didn't feel fear you wouldn't be able to protect yourself from harm. We have a primitive 'fight or flight' reflex which means that when we are in danger we assess the situation and either run away or stand our ground. These emotions have evolved over aeons and affect our thinking and behaviour at a very deep level. For instance, in modern life you may not physically run away (as a hunter in the forest might have done centuries ago); however, your flight response might make you 'shut down' emotionally, or even just go to sleep to avoid pain.

There is a debate among psychologists and others as to whether these behaviours and beliefs are learned (nurture) or innate (nature). My guess is they're a mixture of both: we have evolved into the kind of people we are (size, colour, shape, etc.), and we also have learned from our own individual experience of life. Whatever, feelings have a purpose: they protect you, they keep you in touch with your physical needs (temperature, hunger, thirst, pain, etc.) and, of course, they enable you to form relationships (love, friendship, lust) and to be part of a community (connectedness, communication). We saw in the last chapter that how you are brought up, what kind of family you come from, and how your parents or carers behave or behaved towards you, are all crucial in shaping yourself and also your feelings.

The Nice Person Mindset

As we have seen, if you are a compulsive carer or a codependent you will have learned to put the emphasis on taking care of others at the expense of yourself. The Happy Helper Habit we met in Chapter 1 denies all sorts of feelings and only promotes those which the conscious mind can accept. This is because we have a mental picture of ourselves, a conscious image, which usually drives our behaviour. Psychologists call this a 'mindset'. If you find it hard to say 'no', I think you probably have a Nice Person Mindset. You believe you are a nice sort of person who behaves in a nice sort of way - and your feelings are supposed to follow this belief. They are supposed to be nice. All the time.

Hidden feelings

Unfortunately - or rather, fortunately - we are much more complex than our conscious minds can allow for. Our unconscious mind is like the submerged part of the iceberg lurking under water - about 95 per cent of what goes on in our minds we don't really know about. Thus, we often have all sorts of hidden feelings that we are uncomfortable about acknowledging to ourselves. Our behaviour often gives away our unconscious feelings and motives, in terms of psychological slips and mistakes, although we would hotly deny our feelings if questioned. A typical one is calling your partner by your ex's name: it shows your ex is still in your mind, even though you would probably deny it.

In psychological terms this can be explained by a concept called 'cognitive dissonance'. For instance, if you think you are always generous towards others but find you are feeling very jealous of your best friend's success in getting a pay rise, you will feel a certain amount of emotional conflict. You like your friend, you are happy for her success, but you are also jealous and wish you had her success, too. Being jealous is not something you like to admit to, so you push the feelings down and away. The cognitive dissonance occurs because being jealous does not fit with your image of yourself and therefore with your Nice Person Mindset. If you were entirely nice, would you feel jealous? No. So either you can't be entirely nice (unthinkable, as you want to be nice all through), or you deny your jealous feelings so you can be in a state of 'cognitive assonance' (where everything fits together nicely). Only thing is, when your friend starts having difficulties in her job there's a part of you that secretly says, 'Hooray!' or 'Told you so,' and you might find yourself being less than sympathetic, talking behind her back or even avoiding her altogether to avoid your conflicting feelings. The relationship is soon on the rocks because you have been untrue to yourself, or rather, you've tried to live out a Nice Person role while feeling deeply jealous. The problem is - what do we do with the nasty bits of ourselves that we can't really accept? What happens when we suppress those bits and pretend they aren't there? In fact, bad feelings usually 'leak out' in some way: so we might end up, thinking, saying or doing something 'nasty', which may feel out of character but actually is in character (if we could accept we have both 'good' and 'bad' feelings).

If you don't accept the complexity of your feelings, you can end up behaving in one sort of way (being overly nice to people like your friend, and not saying 'no'). You would probably behave totally differently if you were able to accept all of yourself and your feelings (and be able to admit to feeling jealous or, at least, to admit it to yourself, or even to your friend). If you can't accept the totality of your feelings, it may be because you may be uncomfortable with accepting yourself as less than perfect. For you to say 'no' effectively, therefore, there has to be an adjustment between your unconscious feelings and your conscious mind. Your Nice Person Mindset has to give way to a more complex, true-to-life mental picture of yourself, which includes you having both good and bad bits in your character.

Burying feelings

This can be quite difficult to understand sometimes, particularly without help from a counsellor or therapist, because you may well have learned very early on in life to bury uncomfortable or forbidden feelings to protect yourself from emotional pain and discomfort. You may feel your feelings in a distorted way or have learned to blank them out altogether, if they don't fit in with your Nice Person Mindset, in order to avoid fear and confrontation. You may not be in touch with yourself very much as a consequence. Sometimes we 'project' or push our bad feelings onto another person, blaming them or making them responsible or the bad person, so that we can keep our self-image squeaky clean. Nevertheless, these bad feelings may well leak out in all sorts of ways — 'nasty' thoughts or comments, gossip, avoiding the other person. This is because the feelings don't go away: they get suppressed because we push them down, hoping they will disappear.

Here are two examples of what I mean. First, there is Carolyn, twenty-three, who works as an administrator and lives in a shared house, and second there is Daniel, thirty-seven, who is a middle manager of an administrative office in a large garden furniture firm. Both are trying very hard to be 'nice' people because it fits in with their Nice Person Mindsets: they believe they are kind, thoughtful, friendly, undemanding and well-behaved. They both need to think of themselves as polar opposites of people they dislike - that is, people who are unkind, thoughtless, unfriendly, demanding and ill-behaved. Meanwhile, the truth is much more complex, and we will see that both Carolyn and Daniel contort themselves emotionally to try to fit in with what they believe they are like. What they are *really like,* on an unconscious level, is quite different from what they consciously think they are like.

'I feel guilty saying "no": Carolyn's story

Carolyn, whom we met briefly in Chapter 2, is a musician from a strict Salvation Army background. She's currently taking a break from being a professional violinist to work as an administrative assistant. Rejecting her musical training and career is, in fact, a bit of a silent rebellion against her overweening father, who forced her to play violin from the age of two. Carolyn is a self-confessed 'quiet, shy person' who shares a house with another young woman who works full-time. 'I am unhappy at present with my housemate because she doesn't clean up,' explains Carolyn. 'She doesn't do the washing up or take her turn cleaning and it's driving me mad.' Carolyn finds it hard to say anything about it to her friend. 'I want to be liked and I don't like conflict, but I do feel I'm being taken for granted. I don't say anything directly to her, but I complain to other people. It's got to the point where I am only washing up my own things and leaving hers. She asked me to do the washing up the other day and I didn't say "no", I'd feel guilty saying that, but I didn't say anything. However, I sulked and didn't talk to her for a few days.'

Why won't Carolyn be direct with her housemate? Why can't she say 'no' to an unfair demand to do more washing up when she is already doing more than her fair share? 'I'm frightened of her getting angry with me,' admits Carolyn. 'I hate it when people are angry with me and I suppose I'd rather do anything than cause an upset. It must be something in my past.'

Indeed, Carolyn's father was (and still is) overbearing and self-righteous. 'It was rules, rules, rules at home. Turn the light off, shut the door, sit down, be quiet, sit up straight - God, it was a tense environment.' She got smacked for not saying 'excuse me' when she squeezed past the dining table on her tenth birthday, which she hasn't forgotten because it seemed so unfair and humiliating at the time, and she was always forced to do household chores, play the violin and was forbidden to watch TV. Meanwhile, Carolyn saw her mother being an appeasing doormat. 'She can't say "no" either,' explains Carolyn. 'She goes out of her way to do things for other people. She's very nice and I think she over-compensates for Dad being so difficult.'

Interestingly, Carolyn is beginning to understand that her nice-ness isn't all that nice, since she has started having some counselling to increase her assertiveness. In fact, she is beginning to realise she is quite angry and resentful deep down, hence her anger leaks out in her behaviour towards her housemate. But she doesn't want to believe she is angry, as it threatens her self-image. Nevertheless, she now has inklings that under her Nice Person Mindset lurks something darker and more complex: 'I know that when I agree to do things, I'm not necessarily being nice, I'm being passive,' says Carolyn. Passivity can actually be aggression, albeit heavily disguised: psychologists call this kind of behaviour 'passive aggression', and it means you can grudgingly say 'yes' to something while meaning 'no', or simply resist the other's will by making it extremely difficult for the other person, in a sort of rearguard action. Hence Carolyn's sulking at home or only washing up her own knife, fork and spoon in a pointed way.

Carolyn says she'd love to be able to say what she feels, especially at the time. 'I store it all up and then it all comes out with a big bang later,' says Carolyn. 'I make things up sometimes or pick on things, especially with my boyfriend, but I avoid an all-out fight and apologise all the time afterwards, because I'm scared he'll leave me.'

It is quite common that we will 'dump' our buried or negative feelings on to someone or something that is relatively 'safe'. For instance, Carolyn wants to assert herself with her housemate but feels unsure of the relationship, so picks a fight with her boyfriend instead. He is a safer bet. Even so, Carolyn is frightened that if she is too assertive with her housemate, or even her boyfriend, she will be acting just like her father - that is, like an angry, oppressive, unlikeable person. This would be painful for her, as she would end up behaving in a way she despises and which she is trying so hard to avoid. As a consequence, Carolyn is straining every sinew to never say 'no' or be confrontational - it's the opposite extreme of her father's behaviour. She would suffer from cognitive dissonance if she were like him, so she works hard to retain an illusion of cognitive assonance - that is, being a Nice Person. However, she has flipped to the opposite extreme and become a doormat — although, in fact, not a very nice one. Making things up, sulking, hinting, being passively aggressive are all indirect ways (like only washing up her own things) of trying to get a direct message across. This is all 'leakage' of her bad feelings. The only problem is that this kind of generalised behaviour can be interpreted in many ways - and may even be misinterpreted. If Carolyn could rid herself of the belief that she needs to be a nice person (like her mother) and that being angry doesn't mean she is a nasty person (like her father), then she could begin to say 'no' as and when appropriate. So what could Carolyn say to her housemate? Can she change her own behaviour in the present, regardless of its origins in her somewhat painful past?

And the answer is a resounding 'yes'.

Of course. It's a matter of CHOICE. Carolyn could change now, if she wanted to, and she could use the pain of her past and anger as a motivating fuel to make things better. You don't have to get stuck in the past. You don't have to keep re-enacting it, either. But if you can catch yourself when you do and ask yourself, 'Is this what I really want?' you can decide to act definitely from the next minute on.

Picture this.

Scene: Carolyn and her housemate are both in the kitchen after a hard day's work, with the sink piled high with dirty dishes. Neither are washing up, both are sitting at the table sipping mugs of tea, hardly looking at each other, having shared a few pleasantries about their respective days at work. The atmosphere is tense.

Carolyn: (looking down into her mug for inspiration) I, er, think it's time for us to sort out what we do about the washing up and house chores ... er... um ... I've, er, got a proposal.

Housemate: (*looking up sharply, but interested*) Oh yeah, what's that?

Carolyn: (*blushing, looking frightened, but proceeding bravely*) Well, er, um, it hasn't been working very well, has it? And I've got to admit, I've got quite resentful about you not washing up, which is why I've been doing my own. (*Pause.*) But that's a bit petty, isn't it?

Housemate: (*looking irritated, but still listening*) Umm, so?

Carolyn: (*flushed, but still hanging in there*) I suggest we either take it in turns to wash up from now on, or we simply wash our own things. What do you think?

The point here is not that there is an immediate solution to the problem, but that Carolyn engages in a discussion about it and that she communicates her feelings to her housemate, who may or may not be interested in sorting things out. But what if, as in Carolyn's worst nightmares, her housemate takes up a defensive stance and gets angry?

Housemate: I think you've got a bloody cheek to say you do all the washing up. I do my fair share. Anyway, you're a pain because you're always sulking about something or other.

What can Carolyn do at this point? Defend herself? Protest loudly her innocence? Run into her room, slam the door and sulk some more? Go quiet and look guilty? Or perhaps she can stand her ground, as she could say:

Carolyn: Yes, you're right, you have washed up sometimes and I do sulk. But I do that because I feel angry and that you take me for granted, and to be honest I find it hard to talk about. But I'd like to start again and set up a new system - such as taking it in turns to wash up. There's obviously a difficulty here so what do you think we should do?

Carolyn acknowledges her part in it all (which diffuses her house mate's defensive anger) and owns the problem as *their* problem (so she doesn't just blame her housemate), but she also stands her ground and continues with her quest. Of course, it may not work out and Carolyn may end up moving out (or her housemate may leave). This, in part, would be also down to how much support she got, say, from her boyfriend or counsellor for standing her ground with her housemate. Talking with other trusted people – family members, a counsellor, a partner - can be crucial for success in this kind of one-to-one confrontation with someone who is 'difficult' in your life. It is certainly worth tackling her problems with her housemate, however, because whoever Carolyn lives with next is bound to bring up similar issues, simply because living with other people always does. Running away does not make this kind of problem disappear. She may be lucky to be able to find a good 'fit' in another household or not. So, on an emotional level, it is important that Carolyn analyses why anger paralyses her (she was small, her father was big, she was frightened by his hitting her and his angry outbursts, and she hated the rigid rules regime). She can work this through with the help of a good counsellor and begin to stand her ground, bit by bit. Each time she says 'no', even in a quiet and shy voice, will be chipping away at the fear which paralyses her ability to assert herself.

We will examine and discuss this kind of issue further as we go through the book. As you read, see if you can spot how people behave and why, and think about any parallels in your own life. Do you ever behave in a similar way to make yourself feel comfortable, or at least to maintain a belief in yourself as a Nice Person - that is, the one who is usually in the right and who doesn't create difficulties?

'I can't say "no" to my staff': Daniel's story

The workplace is fraught with feelings for most of us. We spend most of our waking lives at work, and people necessarily come to work loaded up with their personal problems and individual difficulties. Of course, you are paid to do a job, but it's never that simple. The workplace is actually like a microcosm of family life, and we play out roles there which reflect our own family backgrounds as well as our wider life experience. We also play specific job roles at work, and as you progress within a workplace you will probably take on more power and responsibility. How you take to the power and responsibility, and how you use it, will reflect your own personality as well as your feelings about authority. Some people are comfortable leaders. Often they have been the eldest or only child in a family. They are happy with making decisions, taking charge and/ or being responsible. Sometimes people are uncomfortable leaders, and if so, they will have a difficulty with owning and wielding their authority. This can be true of middle or youngest children or of people who have low self-esteem and self-confidence for a variety of reasons.

Daniel, thirty-seven, was the youngest child in a family of three. He had a boisterous older brother and sister and his parents were both career people who were fairly absent, both physically and emotionally. He did fairly well at school and left after A levels, and has worked his way up to a middle management position in a large garden furniture firm. It is a fairly traditional firm, however, and Daniel is in charge of a small team of five, three men and two women. They deal with orders and there is a great deal of paperwork and attention to detail involved. The problem for Daniel is that he finds it hard to say 'no' to his staff. Recently, one of his staff has been using the work computer for extensive personal emails and Daniel suspects he might even be stealing office stationery. However, Daniel is finding it hard to bring the issue up with the staff member involved.

'I should be managing Michael better by confronting him with his behaviour, but I can't seem to bring myself to do it,' explains Daniel awkwardly. 'I suspect he's been abusing the firm in all sorts of ways as I think he's bored in his job, but he's the sort of bloke who will explode if I challenge him, so I guess that's putting me off.' It's very hard for Daniel, as a man, to admit that he might be frightened of a fellow employee, but that is actually the case. We often fantasise about the outcome of a confrontation and see ourselves coming off worse. So why is it so hard for Daniel to say 'no' to someone in his charge? 'Michael and I have never really got on,' explains Daniel, 'and I think he reminds me of my elder brother, Peter, who used to push me around quite a bit. It was boys' stuff, you know, play fighting and that, but I always came off worse and I could never beat him.' Daniel's brother once locked Daniel in the garden shed and the whole family forgot about him until tea-time, thinking he was out with a friend. Daniel's parents told his brother off, but Daniel didn't feel he had the comforting he needed. He was told to laugh it off and be brave.

'I think I feel if I confront Michael he'll somehow run rings round me,' admits Daniel, 'but I think the other staff members know what's going on, and if I don't do something about it, it will soon get back to the boss and then my own job will be on the line.' Daniel also finds it hard to say 'no' to his boss, who is a bit of an old-fashioned dictatorial manager. Daniel has found himself being the filling in a typical managerial sandwich. As a middle manager he needs to find a way of saying 'no' to his employee, not only to do his job but to maintain the respect of his staff, improve his self-respect, and also keep the respect of his boss.

What is it Daniel really fears? 'I think he will try and humiliate me by denying it's true and making a scene in front of the others.' Daniel would rather the problem went away on its own, but it's not going to - at least, not without his intervention. There is also another issue. It is possible Daniel is frightened of his own anger. Sometimes people who seem very timid or docile are, in fact, sitting on a mountain of rage. He may well be fearful of unleashing his rage, which would have a lifetime of unfair feelings pent up in it (such as the childhood shed incident). This is one of the reasons seemingly quiet people run amok with sten-guns in shopping malls - something snaps and a lifetime of repressed rage runs riot. Daniel may be protecting both himself and his staff from his rage - but the cost to him is enormous.

So what can Daniel do? First he needs to understand the feelings which are keeping him powerless at work: fear of not being able to win an argument, possible fear of attack and humiliation (especially in front of others), fear of losing his temper and becoming murderous. Unconsciously, Daniel is back in his family with his elder brother beating him up and his parents (like his boss) not really defending him. The feelings, of being isolated and powerless, are undermining his ability to do his job. He needs, therefore, to separate Michael from his elder brother in his mind and to recognise and accept his feelings. He needs to connect with the fact - in present time - that he is paid to do a job and he has to do it; and that he is now a big grown-up man, not the scared little boy who got locked in the garden shed. We often feel small and vulnerable as if we are still stuck in the situation of our youth, when the reality is that we have now grown up and are far more powerful than we realise.

How should Daniel approach his staff member? First, he needs to get his evidence (print out the email list, check the stock cupboard, etc.). Second, he needs to inform his boss of his suspicions, and make a reasonable plan of action. Third, he needs to get his boss's backing for his plan, and not operate in isolation. Fourth, he needs to confront Michael, alone and in private. To say 'no' effectively to Michael, Daniel has to be in touch with the part of him -the grown-up part - that feels in charge of the situation. He needs to prepare himself to deal with Michael's anger, denial, duplicity, by out-psyching him. In the confrontation, Daniel needs to stick to his own agenda and not let his feelings run the show. This will make him grow as a man and a manager, because psychologically he is outwitting his parents who didn't support him and his brother who bullied him. By winning in the present, he will be laying the painful past to rest.

Daniel: Michael, here's a printout of the emails you have been sending on your computer during lunch-times. What have you got to say about this?

Michael: Nothing. That was Deirdre. She sent them, not me.

Daniel: I know they are yours because you were the only one in the office at the time and they have your number on them. I want you to stop sending emails in work time.

Michael: That's ridiculous - what do a few emails matter? Er, not that I sent them.

Daniel: I'm just letting you know it's not acceptable behaviour. The firm does not allow employees to send emails in work time: it's a sackable offence.

Daniel's knees might be knocking under the table and his mouth might be dry, but he is standing his ground. He is saying 'no' to Michael effectively, and not letting his own feelings dictate his managerial behaviour. His Nice Person Mindset has had to give way to Effective Manager Mindset, and his self-confidence and self-esteem will be boosted should he manage the meeting and Michael's resistance to owning up. Daniel has to be able to be nasty as well as nice. In the above scenario, Michael does not admit, fully, to his email sending and Daniel does not mention the thieving, but Daniel has asserted his managerial authority and it will help him deal with the next round of Michael's misdemeanours, if they continue.

Feelings lead to patterns

Hurtful feelings from the past can be buried and forgotten, but can still run our lives. We probably suppressed them at the time because we did not have enough help to deal with them from those around us. Buried feelings have a tendency to cut us off further from our present-day feelings. Thus, unresolved painful feelings can lead us to develop rigid patterns of behaviour and to have inflexible responses to life. We need to unearth the feelings which were buried long ago and give them voice, or air, so that we can integrate them into our everyday lives. Otherwise, we remain at the mercy of things we don't really understand or know about - like the proverbial iceberg, our feelings can remain 95 per cent submerged.

Like many of us who find it hard to say 'no', both Carolyn and Daniel are operating within the patterns their families and later life experiences bestowed upon them. Both are desperate to be loved and liked, respected and listened to, and yet their very behaviour seems to bring about the opposite. In the first part of this book we have identified the Happy Helper Habit which drives many of us to be overly helpful all the time. Also, we have looked at the more serious emotional addiction to helping and codependency which can make people into compulsive carers and rescuers. In this chapter we have looked at the uncomfortable feelings which can get in the way of feeling you can be true to yourself. Instead of asserting yourself and saying 'no', you can end up appeasing and pleasing, just to keep bad feelings at bay. After all, if you hated your dominant father or mother you will hate yourself for acting like them, so you become a doormat instead.

A doormat is a typical people-pleasing pattern, as we have seen. Here are some other patterns which you might recognise in yourself:

People-pleasing patterns

- **Doormat:** 'Use me, I don't mind';
- **Martyr or Saint:** 'The needs of others must always come first';
- **Diamond or Salt of the Earth:** 'Leave it to me, I'll fix it';

- **Happy Helper:** 'I'll do anything to help - I'm always here at the ready';
- **Cheerful Chappy:** 'Nothing bothers me, I'm fine. Cheer up, it'll never happen.'

Because these people-pleasing patterns are unreal, in that they are only one side of the personality coin, they do not serve the person they drive. You cannot be your true, authentic self if you are always nice and pleasing. It will make your relationships and dealings with people ineffectual and awkward. What's worse, it actually makes you open to abuse and attack. If you want to be a parent or get promoted in your work, if you want mutually loving relationships and satisfying friendships, you will have to accept that there are sides of yourself which are not particularly nice or happy, or helpful or cheerful or self-sacrificing. You will need to get in touch with your *real needs,* your *real feelings and desires* and the *real part of yourself* that knows what it wants in life.

Patterns hook together

Inevitably, people find each other out and their patterns often hook together. Which is why you find love relationships which have a quiescent man with a dominant woman, or a doormat with a bruiser. However, as you become more aware of what it is you do with people or how you operate in life, you can begin to act differently. Many of us repeat our relationship patterns over and over, such as with people who are tough to say 'no' to, or by doing jobs in which we find it difficult to assert ourselves. Sometimes it is because we are trying to re-enact the fight we lost when we were children, so we have a repetitive action replay in adult life. Sometimes, however, we decide to do the opposite of our childhood experiences in reaction to the painful feelings of the past.

Steps to recognising your feelings

Take a moment. Sit comfortably in a chair (notebook and pen nearby). In order to tune in with yourself, try the following:

- Stop, close your eyes, turn your attention internally.
- Register what your body is feeling, or where your attention is at the moment. What are you experiencing? Are you buried in worries in your head? Is there tension in your solar plexus (under your ribs) or in your face? How does your chest feel?
- Allow yourself to feel — and follow the feeling. Notice it. What do you do with it? Do you switch off from it? Do you try to distract yourself? Do you push it away or down? Do you feel irritated by feeling it, or a mixture of feelings, and try to control it or them?
- Stay with the feeling or feelings - can you stay with them long enough to decipher them? Can you allow yourself to feel several, often contrary, things at once? ('I feel sad and happy, angry and relaxed,' etc.)
- Stay with the process - let the feelings bubble up, change, grow, disappear. Let the tears flow if they need to, or perhaps you will laugh or yawn or feel irritated.
- Note down your feelings and any thoughts that go with them.

Do this daily and you will begin to be able to tune in with yourself regularly. All you need to do is stop for, say, five or ten minutes and practise the above exercise. This will give you more power over your life as you are more aware of yourself and your emotional state.

Acting as if...

We have seen that our feelings have their roots in childhood, as do our behaviour patterns, and although they may continue to drive us in adulthood they do not have to rule us for life.

It is possible to understand more about your unconscious feelings and to adopt a new, conscious way of being, to counter what they seem to make you do. Sometimes we simply have to *decide* to *act as if we* are confident, powerful, happy and assertive in order to operate effectively in the world. This is an appropriate point to move to Part 2 of this book so you can start learning how to kick the Disease to Please and, therefore, how to say 'no'.

Part Two

How to Say 'No'

5

Kicking the Disease to Please

Change is always a challenge. It can be scary, but it can also be very exciting. It can be like standing on the top board of a swimming pool - do you jump or will you dive? Or do you go back down the steps, relieved to be safe, on dry land again? Poised on the edge of the diving board you can feel, 'Oh dear, can I really plunge in? What if I hit the water badly?' Similarly, you may be feeling afraid of saying 'no', thinking, 'How will I handle my relationships, my work colleagues, parents, family, friends, husband, kids, if I'm not people-pleasing?' Of course, it is scary, but I would like to offer you the chance to simply hold your nose and jump. *Splash...* the water's actually cool and refreshing - it was a risk, but, boy, was it fun! Obviously, you'll need to think, as you read this book, about what your life would be like if you weren't running yourself ragged or feeling under the cosh of all the things you have agreed, subconsciously, to do or be. Reading this, you might now be feeling, 'Look, my life isn't so bad, I can say "no" sometimes, I don't really need to change that much.' That may well be true. In which case, give this book to a friend who can't say 'no'. However, I have a hunch that this could well be a psychological defence against things changing.

Having been someone who has found it hard to say 'no' - and who still finds it hard from time to time - I can definitely say it is *absolutely possible* to give up having a knee-jerk Happy Helper Habit every time anyone or anything demands something from you. You can decide to give up the Disease to Please just as you can give up any other addictive behaviour (if you want to, that is). What's more, it is certainly possible, and desirable, to stop saying 'yes' when you mean 'no', or 'double-guessing' other people's needs in a desperate desire to please and appease, but it does mean you making some fairly tough decisions about yourself and your life.

I'll be honest, however. Learning to say 'no' effectively will not happen overnight and, as we saw in the first part of the book, there is no magic wand that can be waved to make you suddenly super-assertive and ultra-confident. To suggest that you can learn to say 'no' in seven days would be selling you a phoney pipe-dream, a bit like asking you to don the Emperor's new clothes while learning to dance the flamenco in five minutes. Nonetheless, there are steps you can take once you have decided you are truly fed up with being a 'yes' man or woman.

To begin at the beginning, you need to:

- decide you want to be able to say 'no' more often, especially where you say 'yes' automatically (to keep the peace, to appease, etc.);
- identify the situations where you feel most vulnerable to pleasing people — is it in personal relationships, with friends and lovers? Or with authority figures, like bosses and parents?
- decide to have a go at saying 'no' and expect to feel new or uncomfortable feelings as a consequence. You need to welcome the feelings and accept things may feel a bit awkward and unfamiliar at first.

To this end, the second part of the book is aimed at helping you learn *how* to say 'no' - and *how to say it effectively*. It may take you time to think in more detail about how you approach your life, what you feel and how you behave. You should also have a chance to think more about what you want out of your life, which is connected to your ability to say 'no' to things you simply don't want to do. More importantly, it will be up to you to decide to grasp the nettle of change. This has to be done entirely for your own benefit, nobody else's. *Certainly not because someone else told you to.*

Preparing to say 'no'

I would suggest you use your diary or computer file and spend five minutes every day just making a few notes for yourself. It's a good thing to do early in the morning or perhaps late at night, before bed. Self-help books always ask you to do these sorts of things and you might feel irritated — 'Oh, I don't have time, don't make me do something else, I'm busy enough as it is.' Well, I agree, you don't want to be loaded up with lists and lists of things to do, but it is useful to become conscious of what you are doing and how you feel. This makes the task of keeping a daily record fun. Like Bridget Jones, you can keep a highly personalised daily tally of your ups and downs, successes and failures, on the 'no' front. Even a minimal amount of time writing down what you have said 'yes' or 'no' to, and how it has made you feel, will aid your ability to say 'no' even more when you really want to. Success definitely builds on success.

Personally, I always indulge myself by buying a lovely little notebook with a funky cover and a special pen whenever I start a new project. This time the project is YOU, so it's even more important you treat yourself well if you want to succeed. Keeping notes, in some form, is a way of keeping track. It's a way of talking to yourself. When the pressure is on, it is so easy to 'forget' what you have learned or the insights you have gleaned, unless you write them down. Also, 'reminders' on sticky Post-It-type notes are very effective if you are trying to change the way you behave. You can also use star stickers to remind you — stick them to your computer, the kettle, the phone. When you look at them, it can be a way of reminding you that you have a choice. For instance, if you find yourself agreeing too easily to things over the telephone or by email, you can write a Post-It note that reminds you that you can say, 'I'll think about it,' when someone is pressing you to do something. Simply seeing the star sticker can be a reminder. It may seem unfamiliar, odd or embarrassing to say or do such a thing, so having a 'prompt' or even a 'script' can work wonders (after all, your doorstepper, cold caller, pushy partner, needy friend or bullying boss is also working from their own script — *to make you say yes* to what *they* want).

Thus, the book will go on to look at specific situations where you may be finding it hard to say 'no': in love and sex relationships, with your family and friends, at work, with authority and on the street. We will be looking at how some people have learned to change their behaviour. How have they gone about it, and what has been the result? These are real stories about real people who have also been caught in a complex web of people-pleasing but who have nonetheless decided to give it up - and they have succeeded (or are in the process of succeeding). The aim of telling their stories is to inspire you to action (or inaction, as the case may be).

Why you need to learn to say 'no'

It may be essential for you to give up saying 'yes' for some of the following reasons (there are bound to be more, keep a note of your own insights):

- You are not your true self when you agree to things all the time - you are inauthentic and maybe have a false facade (such as Happy Helper) which you hide your real self behind.
- People don't actually like you more when you say 'yes' all the time, as people-pleasing isn't pleasing (go back to Chapter 2).
- Being nice all the time is not really nice - it can be very insincere, even nauseating (go back to Chapters 2 and 3).
- It may be affecting your physical and mental health, making you feel exhausted, fearful, tearful — leading to 'burnout' (go back to Chapters 1 and 3).
- It may be affecting your relationships, making you feel unhappy, unloved, unsatisfied and resentful.
- You are wasting your energy and your life - because you spend time on inessential things which don't really take you forward.

- If you say 'yes' addictively, you need to give it up so you can get a life (see Chapter 3).
- Nobody respects or likes a doormat, even 'if they want their feet nice and clean.'
- Taking on too much responsibility removes other people's responsibility for their own lives.
- Your own life gets stuck in a rut when you can't say 'no' effectively.

Patterns past their sell-by date

This might seem like a lot of bad news, but it's not really. You are courageous, brave even, in that you are currently looking the Disease to Please in the face, in order to free yourself from its grasp. There is hope. The good news is that through looking at things squarely you can understand how the urge to please people can run and even ruin your life. It can give you a chance to think outside the box. If you have behaviour patterns which have developed in response to negative feelings (as explained in Chapters 1-4), you might well be 'stuck' in an outmoded way of thinking and acting, with behaviour patterns which are well past their sell-by date. Changing your patterns of behaviour will also change your feelings, which in turn will reinforce your self-confidence and change your patterns of behaviour. You will build your self-esteem and self-confidence as you learn that it is not only possible, but actually pleasurable, to say 'no'.

How to kick the Disease to Please

In Part One of this book we identified two main strands of the Disease to Please:

- Happy Helper Habit

and, more seriously,

- Codependency

The difference between these is, to some extent, a matter of degree:

- The Happy Helper Habit is the knee-jerk 'yes' response, whereby you feel it is hard, if not impossible, to say 'no' to someone or something. You want to please and appease and you seem a one-dimensional person (for more on this go back to Chapters 1 and 2).
- Codependency is where you put all of your attention on another person's needs. You spend a great deal of time and energy thinking about and trying to meet their needs, which is a way of controlling the person, although you seem to do this at your own expense. This is an emotional addiction (for more on this go back to Chapter 3).

The outcome of both these types of behaviour - which often, but not always, go together — is that:

- you please people before yourself;
- you need to be needed and loved/liked and feel you have to earn it in some way;
- you find it hard to deny the other person what they want;
- you try to control the other person by putting all of your attention on them;
- you put your own needs last.

If you want to give up the Disease to Please; you will need to start doing the following:

- Put yourself first.
- Give up pleasing people to feel good about yourself.
- Understand that you are not indispensable.
- Take time out to think.
- Communicate what you need and want for yourself.
- Meet your own needs for yourself.

- Let other people articulate their wants and meet their needs for themselves.
- Work out your life goals - and pursue them actively.

The above may seem deceptively simple at first glance, but it will take time and effort for you to reorient your life away from other people's needs towards your own. As we have seen, if you are a people-pleaser, your compulsion will be to worry about and pay attention to others' lives, often as a way of not paying attention to your own life. This will simply have to stop for you to break free of chronic people-pleasing.

Putting yourself first

Most of us have been taught that putting ourselves first is 'selfish' — a word that is extremely pejorative. We use it all the time to denote how horrible, mean and nasty someone is: 'Oh, he's so selfish, he only thinks of himself,' we say of a man who cheats on his wife or of the woman who goes shopping all weekend and neglects the kids. I think we need to make a distinction between being self-centred, narcissistic and thoughtless, which is what 'selfish' tends to mean, and putting yourself first. It is virtually impossible for us to relate to each other as humans if we aren't selfish to some extent. We need to be a definite 'I' meeting another definite 'I', otherwise there is no real connection or communication. However, the person who needs love and wants to appease will be an indefinite 'I' meeting a definite 'I' - and that can make the latter look extremely selfish and the former, selfless. In fact, as we have seen throughout this and earlier chapters, the seemingly selfless person is often pulling the strings in the relationship. So how can you put yourself first without becoming a nasty, self-centred boor? The trick is to know yourself. Self-knowledge will help you understand what you like and don't like, what you want and what you need.

'I can't say what I want': Mandy's story

We all have desires and wishes which are particular to ourselves and which may not necessarily suit someone else. A successful business executive, Mandy, thirty-six, contacted me after reading my article in *Woman*. She had no difficulty in saying 'no' at work, but in terms of her personal life it was a disaster. Mandy had put her career first and been single for most of her teens, twenties and thirties. Now she had fallen deeply in love for the first time, with Bill, a divorcee. Mandy was frightened that she would put Bill off if she was too demanding. 'Because I was so late getting into a meaningful relationship I started off thinking, "I'm going to give it all I've got, I'll agree to everything, I'll do just what he wants."' Because Bill's first wife had been 'difficult', Mandy was even more worried about keeping him happy, so she acquiesced to his ideas about eating out, going away at weekends and meeting other couples. 'It became habit-forming,' Mandy remembers, 'and it was out of character for me, really. I was tough at work and a dormouse at home - it was like I was a split personality.' The strain began to show as Mandy got more and more tense when they tried to discuss arrangements for the forthcoming weekends or holidays. 'I thought it would upset him if I said "no" to going away. He loved coming home and saying, "I've got tickets for this and that," or "Pack your toothbrush, we're off to a hotel."' Mandy felt mean - selfish, that is — because Bill was treating her wonderfully and she didn't want any of it.

'I was always going away to hotels with my work. It was always strange rooms and strange places, and to be honest a real treat for me was to curl up at home with Bill and a good book.' Mandy felt she didn't dare say this to Bill, because she was terrified of losing the relationship. After all, it was the first time she had given her heart to someone and she really wanted the relationship to work. However, Bill was getting a rough ride even though Mandy was seemingly going along with his plans. Her frustration leaked out nonetheless. 'I suppose I couldn't suppress myself totally,' explains Mandy.

'On our weekends away I would be snappy or sulky. I couldn't really hide my true feelings. Bill would say, "Are you happy?" and I'd say, "Yes, of course," but I wouldn't say it sincerely. He knew something was going on, but I couldn't talk about it.'

The crunch finally came after Mandy had been away for a week on business. When she met up with Bill on the Friday night he gave her a glass of wine and said, 'I've got a lovely restaurant booked for eight.' Exhausted and irritable after her week away, Mandy blurted out, 'Oh no, not again,' and Bill was utterly surprised. 'Why ever not?' he asked. Tearfully, Mandy risked all and poured out her heart. She told him how she really felt about whizzing around at weekends. All she wanted was a bit of R and R, rest and recuperation, *at home,* and, of course, to be with Bill. 'I couldn't believe his reaction,' says Mandy. 'He just said, "Why ever didn't you say so? Of course we can stay at home. I wanted to treat you, that's all."' In retrospect it seems so simple, but Bill was desperately trying to please Mandy while she was desperately trying to please him. Her not saying what she really wanted meant their relationship was operating in the dark. 'He was honest, saying he would be gutted if we didn't do some of the things he liked doing, and I said, "I'm sorry you'd feel like that, but I also need to tell you when I don't want to do it."'

The outcome of this story is that they are still together and very much in love. They agreed to be absolutely honest with each other, even if it was awkward. Finally, after some discussion, they came to a compromise of going away sometimes, with plenty of warning for Mandy, and staying home other times. Bill insisted that Mandy put herself first and stop appeasing him, and she insisted that he tell her when he really wanted to go somewhere special for himself, rather than double-guessing what he thought she wanted.

Recently, they visited Bill's family and after lunch everyone wanted to go for a walk - except Mandy. 'I felt panic as I just wanted to curl up with my book when everyone was putting on their wellies. I was amazed when Bill looked at me and winked, and I said, "I'd like to stay here and read, is that OK?" and the whole group smiled and simply said, "Yes, see you later." I didn't realise until then that I could have what I wanted, and Bill waved at me and winked again as he went out.' Afterwards, Bill told her he was relieved that she was finally putting her own needs first. However, it also meant that Mandy wasn't snappy with Bill because she was repressing her needs and pretending to go along with the gang, so she was very loving and warm towards him, having had time for herself. 'I learned that it was absolutely fine for me to do what I wanted to do, although I was brought up with the notion that women generally put themselves second. I certainly never saw my mother get anything she wanted.' Luckily, Mandy has learned that things have changed for women today.

There are many examples of this kind of situation, where we feel awkward about being straight in putting ourselves first. We do it all the time in many different ways, and it actually makes life difficult for others as well as ourselves if we don't articulate our needs. We return to this theme throughout the rest of this book.

Feeling and accepting your feelings

When you stop pleasing people, especially when you have been someone who says 'yes' automatically, to appease and avoid conflict, you may well feel your buried feelings more acutely. Often we please others because we fear, as we have seen in Part One of this book, that others will not like or love us, or - worse - that they will scare or even attack us. Avoiding confrontation and conflict means that you necessarily flatten yourself out when you meet someone else's desires or their resistance. You tell yourself that the other person is more emotional or unstable than you are, that they need x or y more, and that, fine, you can let them have what they want. Often this is done simply to keep the peace.

So when you step out of your doormat, pleaser or appeaser role and begin to voice that taboo word, 'no', you may well feel:

- even more scared that you will get into trouble, be disliked, attacked, even hit, in response;
- strange - who are you when you say 'no' to people?
- embarrassed and awkward - you may say 'no' abruptly or too quietly - because you are simply not used to saying it;
- confused - you may say 'no', then find yourself backtracking rapidly: 'Yes, er, no, yes, no, um, er. .', fearful of what you have done and what the consequences might be;
- angry - why didn't you say 'no' earlier, when it turned out to be so easy in the end? You've wasted years doing things for people, when you could have got on with your own life;
- relieved - well, it was scary to contemplate, but it went quite well and now you feel relaxed;
- proud - you did it, well done! After all this time thinking it was impossible, you did it - your self-esteem will blossom;
- surprised - was it me that did or said that? It's not in character. Who am I when I say 'no' and stand up for myself? Who will I be if I continue this way - will I become selfish, insensitive and boorish?

As we saw in Chapter 4, feelings are there for a purpose. They actually keep us alive, they allow us to feel our sensations (pleasure as well as pain) and without them we'd be as inanimate as a lump of rock. You need to make friends with your feelings. Allow yourself to have a whole spectrum of emotion - notice how you feel not only day to day, but hour to hour, moment to moment. Jot down in your diary, make an entry on your computer file — notice all the nuances of emotion you experience, the full range, how they change and how you feel. No, you won't go mad, but, yes, you will start feeling all those feelings you have squashed down in the hope of being eternally nice and good.

Take a meditative moment...

Take a moment, right now, to feel. Take a deep breath, take the breath right down inside yourself, then, after reading this paragraph through, close your eyes. Listen to your breathing for a few minutes (you can set the alarm clock for five or ten if you like). As you breathe in, think 'rising', and as you breathe out, think 'falling'. Feel your breath coming in and out and listen to your mind saying 'rising' and 'falling'. Keep doing this until you feel very calm and quiet or until your alarm goes off. Keep your eyes closed and ask yourself, 'What am I feeling?' Can you feel any feelings at all? Is there tension in your solar plexus or your jaw? Do you feel sad or happy, tense or calm, or a mixture of all of these? Perhaps you are hungry or thirsty, maybe you are angry about something that happened earlier, or worried about or preoccupied with something. Sit quietly, just for a few minutes, and watch your thoughts coming and going. Tune in with yourself and let your feelings just be.

I meditate daily, and what I have just described is like a basic meditation. I often find tears running down my cheeks while I meditate, as a sad thought or feeling surfaces. I don't worry about it, I notice it, it releases naturally and I carry on sitting. I find fifteen minutes of meditation a day is quite wonderful, especially when I am hurried, overloaded and stressed, and especially when I feel out of touch with myself. We seldom get time just to stop and sit, as most of us are simply on the go, 24/7. You can benefit hugely from a few minutes of quiet time, as your brain waves and heart rate slow right down. It allows your feelings to be felt and time to expand - something which is crucial for us in our hectic lives.

Don't try and rid yourself of your feelings or squash them down. Simply notice them. Why is this important? When you say 'yes' automatically or spend your life pleasing others you are often completely out of touch with yourself. This means you can actually cause yourself physical or emotional harm because you don't know what you really feel or what you want. By agreeing to do something for someone when you don't want to, you put yourself under stress. If you are in touch with your feelings you are in a position of power over your own life and will. The problem is, so many of us are run ragged in a world that does not go at a human pace, that we say 'yes' before we think. Can you do that one extra thing? 'Yes, that's fine,' and you reach for a sixth cup of high-caffeine coffee to keep you going while you do it. If you took a moment, tuned in with yourself and asked, 'What do I really want?' you might find yourself thinking, 'Oh, I don't really want to do that. I want to get some rest, or go swimming, or go home, or go to bed.' Then you have a sense of yourself and how you are feeling, and it is far easier to say 'no'.

Taking your moment

Now you might be thinking, 'It's all very well to say take a few moments and tune in or meditate for fifteen minutes, but I can't do that at the office or at home, with the kids round my feet.' Well, you can. I even go to the toilet and sit on the seat for five minutes and tune in; I sit on a train or bus, eyes closed, tuning in; I put a video on for my daughter, go out into the garden or have a quick bath, and tune in for ten minutes. I start the day tuning in because when I don't the day seems more rushed and out of kilter. The phone goes and I'm saying 'yes', 'yes', 'yes' before I've thought or felt what makes sense for me. I did this the other day and agreed to teach a writing class at my daughter's school on a day I was taking an exam. Well, I'm sure there were all sorts of unconscious things going on - I certainly didn't want to do an exam - but I said 'yes' instantly, because I wanted to please the teacher who was asking and wanted to show what a good, participative mummy I was. So I had to phone back and backtrack. Instead, I could have said, 'I'll think about it,' or 'Let me check my diary and get back to you,' and certainly, if I had taken my moment that day and tuned in more with myself, I probably wouldn't have double-booked myself.

Try it. Just once will make a difference. Take a moment, especially sitting in a traffic jam when you want to scream at the cars all around or feel like ramming them with yours, or when you are running late. Ask yourself - am I doing what I really want to be doing? Can you phone and say, 'I'm late, I'll be there in half an hour,' and then spend three minutes sitting still and calming down? Accept your feelings - a whole wide range of them, including the so-called 'bad' ones as well as 'good' ones - and you will be halfway to saying 'no' effectively in your life. Feeling your feelings is like getting exercise. You'll feel the benefit if you keep doing it little and often. Ask your partner or best friend to ask you, 'How do you feel?' and give yourself a few seconds to feel before you answer. Your feelings can be all jumbled up: 'I feel annoyed and happy' or 'sad and relaxed' — there is no right answer. However, knowing what is going on in you is very powerful and will enable you to put yourself at the centre of your own life.

Stop worrying what other people think about you

In life, some people you meet will like you, others will not. You'll get on really well with some, and never really 'click' with others. People-pleasers spend a great deal of time worrying what other people think about them and then try hard to get themselves liked. Well, give it up. It's fruitless. The harder you try to be liked, the less likeable you probably are. Why? People can smell sincerity. And insincerity. People quite like someone gritty or tough, someone to push up against. A 'yes' person can feel like a wobbly jelly, whereas someone who knows what they want will feel pleasantly firm to the touch. If someone tries hard to make you like them, it's easy to feel their sweetness is saccharine, rather than genuine. Bending over backwards to be helpful means you can appear one-dimensional. It may be an appropriate role to play if you are a waitress or airline check-in person because you are working to a company script, but in real life you need to get real. So give up worrying what people think about you. They can only get to you if you let them. Who cares what others think, really? What matters is that you like and respect yourself and you have the love and respect of a few trusted people in your life. Confidence comes from knowing that fame, the adoration of the many, counts for nothing. It's a very lonely place. But intimacy and genuine love, from the few, is the best fuel for building your self-esteem and self-confidence. Care about the many and you will be all over the place. Care about what you think about yourself and what the few think: this will enable you to know who you are and what you want.

Hopefully, you may naturally evolve to the point where you can say 'no', or rather, not agree to everything. The trick is learning HOW to say 'no' - what works and what doesn't, and what tools you have available to you in your repertoire. We will look, in the next chapter, at the practical techniques available to you when you want to say 'no'.

6

How to say 'no'

My five-year-old daughter can say 'no' extremely effectively. If she doesn't like something or someone, or doesn't want something, she says 'no': simple, unequivocal, from the heart. She says 'no' without fuss and she doesn't explain: 'no' is simply 'no'. The so-called 'terrible twos' that children go through when they begin to separate psychologically from their mothers and carers is when the 'no' word starts to be practised - a lot. Many parents dread this time, although, in fairness, it is an extremely important time for a child emotionally. They begin to understand where 'I' begins and 'you' (Mummy/Daddy/carer) ends. Toddlers, being small and powerless in relation to the adults around them, have to make their feelings felt. 'No' is exercised, literally, in tantrums, tears, emotional storms and stamps of the feet. It is as if 'no', as a word, is not enough. Toddlers' whole vocal range, their physical and emotional selves, have to be thrown into the 'no', too. They have to make an impact — and they do.

One of the reasons adults find the 'no' phase so difficult in two-year-olds (and older kids, and especially teenagers, of course) is that many of us had the 'no' repressed or beaten out of us. Lots of our 'no's' have simply gone unnoticed or unheard. Going back generations, the rules of parental engagement were stricter and the belief that children's desires and wishes should be listened to was virtually non-existent (the Victorian notion of children being 'seen and not heard' surprisingly lives on through our experience of our families and parents). It's a fairly modern idea to allow children some power or say over their lives. Of course, you can't let a toddler rule the roost, and firm boundaries are essential, but parents need to be able to welcome a toddler's 'no' as the first sign of them beginning to become themselves, psychologically speaking.

No doubt a child saying 'no' brings up all sorts of feelings in the adult: 'We weren't allowed to say "no" when I was young, we had to respect our elders and betters,' or simply, 'What a cheek, who's in charge around here?' or even, 'For goodness sake, I haven't got time for all this, do as I say or I'll get really angry.' These heartfelt cries come usually from people who have found it very hard to have what they want in their own lives and feel almost envious that children should have more choice over theirs. Parents are also fantastically stressed out, trying to balance work, life, home, health, money and their relationship - so allowing a child to flex their will and say 'no' can seem outrageous. However, the world has moved on and psychological knowledge and emotional literacy (understanding how our emotions work) has evolved. We know now that for people to be fairly well balanced in adulthood (or as well balanced as possible), learning to say 'no' and learning to be your true, and separate, self is essential for being able to form relationships and living a productive and happy life.

Saying 'no' in relationships

If you weren't allowed to say 'no' ever as a child, and therefore had to repress your wishes and wants, you will probably find it extremely hard to do so in adulthood (or you may have gone to the opposite extreme and become an all-out rebel with - or without - a cause). How hard it is for you to say 'no' will depend on how you feel about who you are saying it to. In the next few chapters we will be looking, in more detail, at everyday scenarios involving lovers and spouses, family and friends, work colleagues and the people we meet every day and on the street. Some general points are worh noting here, however. How easy or difficult you will find it to say 'no' will depend on your own personality, your experience of life and the type of relationship you have with someone. For instance, some people:

- find it relatively easy to say 'no' to someone on the street who pushes in front of them in a queue, while others find themselves mute in this kind of situation;
- are tough at work, able to bark orders and make decisions all day and yet are sheer dormice, agreeing to everything, with their nearest and dearest.
- find it hard to say 'no' to anyone, near or far, and do everything by mute acquiescence or by distant means (letter, email, text).

What are you like?

What are you like? Who are you really? How do you operate in the world and in relationships? Take a moment to think about yourself. Are you a quiet, shy and introverted kind of person, who would hate to make a fuss in public and can find it difficult to confront others? Even so, you might be quietly confident one-to-one, and be able to say 'no' to someone close because you feel more sure of your ground. Or perhaps you are more outgoing, loud and extroverted and could confidently say 'yes' in public, but are perhaps more shy in private, where you have to be more intimate or where it matters more.

One way of thinking about what kind of person you are and how you operate is to think whether you would be more comfortable saying 'no':

- face to face;
- by telephone;
- by email;
- by letter;
- by texting.

The more distant and detached the means of communication (such as email, letter, and text message), the more introverted, quiet and shy you probably are. When you say 'no' using these means you are usually protecting yourself from the immediate emotional fall-out of your message. You don't want to see the hurt or upset or irritation, and you probably don't want to deal with it either. When we say 'no' to someone this way, we may be protecting ourselves. Perhaps we fear the other person's disappointment, attack or even violence, or perhaps we feel we can say it more cleanly at a distance. You need to think about the implications of saying 'no' this way. In some cases it is wholly appropriate, such as an email message offering you something you don't want to buy - 'No, thank you' or simply a 'delete' will do. But ending a relationship by fax, as Phil Collins did when he told his wife he wanted a divorce? Well, that says something more about him as a character - he probably couldn't bear the emotional confrontation which would inevitably make him feel bad, guilty, ashamed, and so on. Some people would call this kind of 'Dear John' fax cowardly. Clearly, he didn't want to face the emotional flak.

When you say 'no' face to face it can become a confrontation and you may fear the consequences. If it is 'no' to something neutral or simple, it will probably not be that problematic. Where it gets complicated is where there are strong feelings involved or a lot is at stake. If your boss calls you into their office and asks you to work late, and you want to say 'no' because you have a previous dinner date arranged, you will have to find a diplomatic way to say 'no', or at least to handle the situation. However, if someone accosts you in the street and demands your wallet or tries to sell you something on your doorstep that you really don't want, then a strong, unequivocal 'no' is needed (with an eye to keeping yourself safe and escaping the scene as quickly as possible).

Buying time

If you suffer from the Disease to Please, 'yes' will pop out of your mouth, as we have seen, before you can say Jack Sprat. You have learned to appease and to please and the Happy Helper Habit will pop up, like a veritable Jack-in-the-Box, and spout, 'Yes, that's fine,' before your brain engages. In combating the Disease to Please and learning to say 'no' effectively, you have to learn to buy time. You need to understand that something has made you either acquiesce silently (and resentfully) or jump in and volunteer your help, and that your Happy Helper Habit is well past its sell-by date in terms of being useful in your life. You have to buy time: time to think, time to work out what you want, time to get in touch with what you feel BEFORE you say anything at all.

How to buy time

If someone asks me to do something and I don't want to, I find it an extremely good technique to say, 'Thanks for asking me, can I think about it?' (My ex-husband was very good at saying 'maybe' to my proposals and leaving a decision hanging. It bought him time, but it was not really a 'no'. He was really thinking about it.) You can buy time, seconds, minutes, a day, a week, this way. This is especially important if you find yourself saying 'yes', then wanting to backtrack immediately. Backtracking can be very embarrassing as, although it is not impossible to reverse a decision, it will leave the other person feeling you are difficult to deal with, or just plain indecisive, or even ditzy. If you are on the phone and someone is pressing you into a decision, you can say, 'Can I call you back?' and get their number and name, if you don't know it. Give yourself the time and space you need to work out what you want. It may be clear, within ten minutes or an hour, that 'yes', you want to comply, or 'no', you don't. Sometimes this is doubly confusing when you really want to do or take what is on offer, but you know you shouldn't - such as go out for a late meal when you are tired and need an early night, or go shopping with a friend when you are broke. 'I'd love to, but let me think about it,' buys you valuable time just to get in touch with what you really feel. You may find, once the pressure from the other person's presence or seductions is removed ('Go on, you know you want to'), that you can think more clearly - 'No, I don't fancy that.' Then you have to work out just how to communicate your 'no' for maximum effect.

Ways of saying 'no'

Whether you are introverted or extroverted, or whether you are at work, at home or with a new lover, learning *ways* of saying 'no' is important. There are different sorts of 'no' that can be used in different situations, and it is useful to look at what they are before we start tackling real-life scenarios in the next few chapters. Take time to think about your own life as you read. Which ways do you usually say 'no'? Do you say 'no' to a friend by *not* saying it at all? For instance, she says, 'Fancy going to the cinema tonight?' and you reply, 'I think I'm staying in and watching TV. You aren't really saying 'no', but you are implying a 'no'. We are often indirect, and our communications can become confused as a consequence. As we have seen, fear of the other person's reaction, and fear of hurting or offending, are often at root. Also, not knowing what you really want or need can lead to this kind of indirect hinting. I suggest that it helps our relationships greatly, on all fronts, the more unequivocal and straightforward we can be. This doesn't mean being rude, but it does mean being clear.

Five 'no' techniques

If you feel saying 'no' is difficult, here are some techniques which might help (if you can think of any more, jot them down in your diary).

1. Cracked record technique

This can be done face to face or on the phone. It is useful when you are talking to somebody who won't take 'no' for an answer. This can happen with a family member, someone selling you something, your boss or colleague, a domineering lover - anyone else who wants to persuade you to agree to something and who thinks that if they keep going long enough you'll eventually give in. If you usually find yourself saying 'yes' to keep the peace when you want to say 'no', then think about the following:

Scenario: You have volunteered to organise the office Christmas party with three other colleagues. You get a call just as you are leaving the office for a quiet night in. You've been out the last three nights and are tired and somewhat broke, so you really don't want to go out again. You really need to go home and attend to paying your bills, tidying your flat, feeding the cat and having an early night.

Colleague: Hi, I need to ask you a big favour. We're meeting up in the pub after work to go through the last-minute party details. We really need you there as you said you'd take on organising the disco. Can you come?

You: Sorry, I really can't, I'm busy this evening.

Colleague: That's a real shame. You know it's only two weeks to go till the party and there's so much to do. If you don't come, we might not get it all done. Can't you come for a while?

You: I am definitely doing my bit for the party and the disco's well in hand, but I really can't come tonight.

Colleague: Listen, I'll buy you a drink. You only have to stay half an hour. Fiona and Peter are there already getting them in. They said they really wanted you to come - you're so good at organising things. Come on, you'll enjoy it when you get there - and you can leave as soon as we've sorted out the disco business.

You: (try and smile as you speak, as it warms your voice)
Look, I'd love a drink and I'm pleased you think I'm
good at organising, but I really can't come tonight - I'll
come next time. I promise I'll get back to you tomorrow
about the disco - don't worry, it's fine. Enjoy your drink.

The cracked record technique is very effective against
someone who is insistent and persuasive. They want to wear
you down. It might be someone selling religion on your
doorstep or a new date trying to get you into bed. You simply
keep restating 'no'. You don't get into long explanations and
you don't agree to something. You keep saying 'no' until they
eventually get the message and the cracked record has played
out. Looking back at the above, you just kept saying 'no' and
you kept your head. How you say it is important, too. You
might need to pretend to get angry, or actually get angry and
tougher if they go on and on at you relentlessly: 'Look, I've
told you three times, I'm not coming. Got it?' But you would
probably say this to someone who was really annoying you
and with whom you didn't have to have an ongoing work
relationship. You might be more assertive, even aggressive,
towards someone who is telephone selling or trying to pick
you up in a bar. Saying 'no' repeatedly in this way means
you eventually get your message across. The other person
may not like it - but you have persisted in sticking to what
you want to do and you haven't offended anyone. The other
person will probably respect you more, even though they feel
a bit annoyed or upset that you didn't comply. Never mind,
you'll more than make up for it when you've had time to
yourself to relax.

2. Sandwich technique

When someone with whom you have a fairly new or formal
relationship asks you to do something, face to face or on the
phone, it can be a delicate matter to turn them down while
keeping them sweet. Sometimes you will sense that they
will be offended by you saying 'no' outright, or that they

will become difficult, even aggressive, if you do. You might use the sandwich technique with a new acquaintance, an elderly relative or with someone you feel needs some delicate handling by you for whatever reason.

You sandwich a firm 'no' between two positive utterances. For instance:

> *You:* Thanks for asking me to work with you on the project. I'm afraid I'm booked up at present, but perhaps you could call next time you need my help?

Or,

> *You:* I was very touched you invited me, but I can't make it that evening. Hope you have a very nice evening.

This is called psychological stroking. You stroke the person you are talking to, psychologically speaking, both before and after your negative response. The aim is to cushion the blow but to stick to your firm 'no'.

3. Reverse sandwich technique

Sometimes you need to start with a definite 'no' and then cushion it with something nice in the middle, followed by a further negative to reinforce your point. This might be useful if you have staff working for you, or you have a family member or friend who is particularly difficult to get through to, because they always want to have their way. This is definitely more assertive than the sandwich technique, and may be good to use at work meetings or with encounters with difficult people or intrusive strangers. The 'no' comes first, so you make a clear statement, but you stroke them psychologically in the middle of the statement to sweeten the bitter pill. For instance:

> *You:* No, I really can't make it to the meeting. I'm extremely sorry as I would like to be there, of course, but

I hope you have a productive meeting. *The answer's no, I'm afraid.*

4. 'No, but...'technique

Offering an alternative proposal can be a very effective means of saying 'no' to someone's idea. 'Would you like to come back to my place?' is a great idea; perhaps part of you wants to, but it is the first date or maybe it's a new friend, who lives miles away. You can say, 'No, but let's meet again next week,' or 'No, but would you like to go and have a pizza? I know a great place nearby.' If you are not sure of the situation or what you really want, then resort to the cracked record, sandwich or reverse sandwich techniques above. You might find the 'no, but...' technique is really useful with a good friend or family member who is pressing you to meet them or come to something that you really don't want to or simply can't make. You can also use it for everyday choices: 'Would you like wine or beer?' someone asks when you visit. You're driving and you don't want to be rude: 'Thanks, but, no, I'm driving. Could I have water/tea/coffee instead?'

5. Blunt 'no'

I used to run counselling workshops equipped with huge cushions and baseball bats. We used to do a great deal of work on expressing our anger, and I was always delighted at this part of my workshops when a granny with grey hair would beat the living daylights out of a big cushion with a baseball bat, screaming 'NO' at the top of her voice and being beet red in the face. Few of us ever get to vent our pure, undiluted rage. It's absolutely great to do, I can tell you. It obviously isn't appropriate to shout 'NO' and wield a bat at work or on the bus (no matter how much you might want to), but it is good to feel that, when outraged, you can be in touch with a primitive part of yourself that can shout 'NO'.

I would really encourage you to try this in private. 'No' is such a powerful word, and the experience of really voicing it can be wonderful. Make sure you're alone, it's daytime and you are fairly well sound-proofed. You can use something like a bat, cricket stump, piece of bamboo, even just a shoe or your bare hand. Get a big cushion or pile of pillows and, wearing loose clothing, have a go at hitting the cushions or pillows and shouting 'no'. First of all think of someone or something, maybe a recent incident, where you have felt outraged. Picture it in your mind. See yourself in the situation and say 'no'. As you say 'no', hit the cushion. Keep saying 'no' and each time hit the cushion. Keep the 'no's' coming and say 'no' louder and louder each time. Keep going, don't give up, even if you feel silly or embarrassed or feel you are not allowed to be loud. Feel what is going on in your solar plexus, chest, shoulders, or jaw. Can you feel tension? Pain? Do you feel tearful? Keep bashing and try and let out a shout - a bloodcurdling 'NOOOOOO' would be great.

Another technique is to grab a small cushion or pillow, hold it to your face with two hands, bury your face and scream a wild 'nooooo' into the cushion. Allow yourself to breathe between screams, but sometimes doing two or three loud ones into the cushion will release a lot of rage and pent-up aggression. The cushion absorbs the sound well, so you can really let rip (and you won't frighten the neighbours or your family). Only thing is to remember to keep breathing between shouts. This is very effective, because the physical feeling of shouting into something pressed against your face can help release the feelings.

I have done this many times myself and ended up a sweaty, shaking, pulpy mess, very tearful and relieved. It can feel wonderful to feel the roar of 'NO' coming out of you - 'NO, how dare you!' (stamping your foot), 'No, go away.' These basic 'no's' are essential, especially for women, older people and young people, who tend to face all sorts of situations every day which require a blunt 'no'. If you are in touch with a part of yourself that can say this kind of 'no', you are more powerful in your life and in the world, and can protect yourself and others more effectively.

For instance, I was in the park some years ago - a chill winter's afternoon — with my daughter, who was then five. A very big boy, probably around fifteen, came up, and I felt the hairs on the back of my neck stand up. He was watching her strangely as she enjoyed herself on a big tyre swing. She was giggling and happy as she spun round in the sun at exactly the right speed for her. Suddenly, without warning, the boy lunged forward, past me, and spun her very violently, swinging her round so the tyre was going at high speed. Her face registered fear and she cried out. I stepped forward, grabbed the tyre and shouted a very loud 'NO' at the boy, who smirked at me and tried to lean forward again to swing the tyre. I felt a slight panic, but my motherly instincts were to the fore and I glared at him and shouted a very loud and blunt 'NOOO' at the top of my voice. The tone and volume of my voice had got through to him and he skulked off, not saying a word. My daughter looked utterly surprised, as I have never shouted at her although I have said firm 'no's' to her. She was clearly scared, but she was also relieved that I had been strong enough to stand up to a playground bully preying on small girls. I explained to her what I had done and why and we then continued playing, at the speed she liked, on the tyre.

I felt quite shaken afterwards at how aggressive I had been, but I could feel pure anger coming out. At the same time, I felt very gratified and relieved that I had stood up to the boy and sorted out the situation, which could have become very ugly if I had not been 'big enough'. I hate to think what might have happened if I hadn't been there. But I also am pleased that my daughter saw me, her mother, being tough and effective, saying a big 'no'. I think I left an impression that you can't mess with Mum. This, hopefully, will stay with her as a strong and effective role model in her own life.

Of course, we always have to judge a situation finely and you may simply need to walk away rather than say anything. Maybe like Mr. Polly in H.G. Wells' novel, *The History of Mr Polly*, you need to say 'little dog' to get out of awkward situations. He escaped all sorts of scrapes by pointing out of the window or door and saying 'little dog' charmingly and exiting stage left. You can certainly confuse the enemy when you spout gobbledegook. You have to assess the person who is hassling you or persisting with something. A blunt 'no' will work wonders and will say more than gushing sentences of explanation if you need to end a conversation or an encounter. I use it all the time with doorsteppers or people clutching clipboards who stop me on the street.

> *Doorstepper or clipboarder:* Hello, have you got a minute, I have a something here ...?

> *Me:* assessing the situation in a flash, but smiling and saying a blunt 'No, thank you' as I close the door firmly or walk past briskly.

> Encounter over.

> Done and dusted.

Rule of thumb with this kind of situation: if you want to get away, just say a blunt 'no'. Stand your ground, stick to your guns, keep saying 'no', even if the paparazzi are following you down the street or someone is trying to get you to sign something you don't want to sign. 'No' works wonders, especially if said with force, straight eye contact and a loud, firm voice. We will go into this more in Part Three of this book, when we think about what to do in specific life situations.

6. Light/funny 'no'

It may be a quirk of English humour, but a light/funny 'no' can be very effective if you want to get out of a ticklish situation. You have to think Monty Python a bit here. You can say 'no' as if you are saying 'yes', but you actually mean 'no'. Say it with a smile, an ironic look, a nod of the head.

This is particularly effective if someone is not listening to you properly: your partner, or a shop assistant. 'No' said lightly, humorously, with mercurial wit, will convey your feelings because it is really acting in the opposite way to the message. If you are a quick thinker, you can make the situation into something quite entertaining and carry the person you are turning down along with you. You make friends, not enemies this way. However, this does take a bit of nerve and some practice.

Waiter: Would you like some more tea?

You: (smiling, and being light) No, I wouldn't, especially if it was as cold and tasteless as the first cup. But thanks for offering.

You don't have to be rude, although it is a tad sarcastic; however, you will get your point across in a way that is very unequivocal. TV series like *Friends* use this kind of light irony a great deal to good effect. People say 'no' as if they are saying 'yes' and the audience rolls in the aisles. It is definitely an effective way to get a negative message across.

And finally...

The first two chapters in Part Two have been looking at how to kick the Disease to Please and, therefore, how to say 'no'. I would just like to reiterate some basic principles before we move on to look at more detailed scenarios from everyday life.

Don't forget

- You have every right to say 'no'.
- Saying 'no' isn't rude or impolite, it is definite.
- People will respect you if you say 'no'.

- You will like yourself more if you can learn to say 'no' and say it effectively.
- You can make an alternative proposal, even if you turn something down.
- You may respect other people's 'no's' more when you say it yourself.
- The old women's lib adage still holds true: 'Whatever we wear, wherever we go, 'yes' means 'yes' and 'no' means 'no'.'
- You don't have to say 'yes' when you mean 'no'.
- Even if you say 'yes', you can change your mind to a 'no' when you've had time to think.
- It's fine to say 'no'.

Part Three

Saying 'No' in Everyday Life

7

Saying 'no' in love and sex relationships

When you fancy someone or fall in love, it is entirely natural to want to please them. They'll probably (hopefully) want to please you, too. Just think of all the love lyrics you know, such as: 'Baby, I'll do anything for you, I'll give you everything, take my all,' or even just 'Use me.' When we're in love, or even just in lust, we often want to give all of ourselves in a boundaryless kind of way, and consequently it can be extremely difficult to say 'no' to the object of our desire. However, much as you want to say 'yes, yes, yes' to your loved one, there will be times when you need to say a definite 'no, no, no'. Love, passion, desire and lust are central to our experience of being human. Without these feelings the world would simply not go round, as we wouldn't reproduce ourselves as human beings. So love and sexual desire bring up deep, primitive emotions in most of us, male or female. Whether you are attracted to the opposite or the same sex (or both), loving another person brings with it a risk. We all yearn to be understood, accepted, loved for ourselves, but the risk in loving someone else is that they might reject or abandon us. We might not be good enough, not attractive enough, clever enough, lovable enough - or able to love enough. Because of this, saying 'no' in love and sex relationships can feel problematic, if not impossible. To summarise, we might find it hard to say 'no' to someone we fancy, love or are involved with because:

- we want to be liked by them;
- we don't want to be abandoned;

- we fear that if we show them our true selves they will not like us and will leave us;
- we want to please them (and therefore seduce or keep them interested);
- we want to make them happy (even at our own expense);
- we fear what would happen if we said 'no', which seems negative or confrontational (and unromantic).

Dating and mating

When we date someone we are usually on our best behaviour, obviously trying to impress. We want our new partner to like us, so we usually dress up and/or groom ourselves and try hard to be interesting, witty, fun and attractive. You may find yourself wanting to 'treat' them by paying for everything, or may expect them to pay for you (for more on this money minefield, see my book *Stop Fighting About Money: How Money Can Make or Break Your Relationship* - available on Amazon). If you suffer from the Disease to Please, dating can be a nightmare, because you will probably be drawn to trying to please and appease your potential new partner. You may want them to like you so much that you find it difficult to be real with them, as saying 'no' can seem very negative with someone you don't know well. Your date might suggest ten-pin bowling or eating Thai food, both of which you hate, but you don't want to appear boring or unsophisticated so you might agree to go (loathing every minute). At what point do you risk being yourself? How do you turn something or someone down without offending them or driving them away? In actual fact, saying 'no' early on (after first impressions) can be very sexy because it shows a certain confidence, not rudeness. It's a good idea to start getting real with people as soon as you can on a first date. This means there is no great let-down later when the gory truth about you is revealed to the other person.

Practise saying 'no'

Try this short exercise. You can do it with a friend or your current partner if possible, or someone you feel safe with. If you are someone who finds it hard to say 'no' it's a good idea to practise saying it and monitor what feelings it arouses in you. We saw in Chapter 4 that we often protect ourselves from feeling embarrassing, frightening, awkward or angry emotions - those we think of as negative - so we often appease and please instead of saying 'no'. Set aside about twenty minutes and take it in turns, about ten minutes each (you can use a timer if you want).

- First, sit opposite each other (about a foot apart) and get the other person to ask a favour of you (they should ask it nicely, charmingly). They could ask something like 'Could you possibly lend me five pounds?' or 'Could I borrow your car?' or 'Can I come round and, talk about my problems tonight?'
- After you've been asked the favour, look them in the eye and say 'no'. Don't add anything, just say 'no'.
- After each 'no' take a minute to monitor how you feel. How does your body feel? Do you want to look away, or down? Is it scary, tense, awkward, exciting, easy?
- Ask yourself, what did saying 'no' mean to you? Did you want to say something else? If so, what?

Notice all your feelings as you go and jot them down, if it's helpful. Then swop with your partner and let them do the same exercise. Note how you feel when they say 'no' to your request. This should help you begin to identify what saying 'no' to a partner means to you and why it can feel so difficult.

Saying 'no' in love

There are many things you may need to say 'no' to in love: you may not want to date someone or see them again. How do you do this? Do you avoid them when they phone or txt? Do you write them a letter or simply fail to turn up to your next date? We find it very hard to be direct with people, especially if we are going to hurt them, but generally it is a good idea to be as straight as you can be face to face, or at least voice to voice. You may fear doing this because you fear having to deal with their upset, anger, disappointment or pain. You may even fear they could become violent. If you really think this is an issue, then you are probably best taking a friend with you or doing it by phone or letter. However, most relationships are not violent, and you will gain more self-respect and self-confidence if you are able to tell someone directly, albeit diplomatically, that you are no longer interested in them, or even that you no longer love them.

Sandwich technique

You can use the techniques we found in Chapter 6 to say 'no' effectively. For instance, if you know someone loves you more than you love them, and you want to end the relationship regardless, you can use the sandwich technique:

> *You:* I really like you and I've enjoyed going out these past six months. But I have to say, it's not really working for me. I want to end our sexual relationship, but I hope we can still be friends, as I really value you as a person.

You can add in other genuine and positive things, such as their good qualities as a person or the fact that you have had fun together.

Reverse sandwich technique

You can also employ the reverse sandwich technique, especially if you feel you need to be tougher.

> *You:* It's over. I'm sorry, because I've enjoyed our times together, but for me it's definitely over.

Of course, this may not work straight away and there may be some discussion, even an argument, but you are trying to let the other person down, with some psychological stroking.

Blunt 'no' technique

If your soon-to-be-ex is aggressive or argues with you or won't take 'no' for an answer, you might have to resort to a blunt 'No':

> *You:* I'm sorry, but it isn't working for me. It's over, and there's no going back.

Cracked record technique

If your partner protests, you just keep saying 'no', or something similar, in the cracked record technique.

> *You:* I'm sorry, I don't want to go out with you any more, it just isn't working for me.

Repeat this, and variations on the theme, but don't get embroiled in justifications, arguments (especially if you've both been drinking alcohol) or a fight. If you are face to face, then you need to leave physically if they won't take your 'no' as your answer. Ending a relationship, even a short one, is always a difficult 'no' to say. If you can do it properly and with some integrity, you will gain from it long term. The times you do it by fact or by avoiding someone will stay with you as cowardly incidents you are not proud of. Hopefully, most situations within relationships which require a definite 'no' can be resolved in a fairly amicable way.

Saying 'no' when living together and in marriage

There are many situations where one or the other of you needs to say a definite 'no'. It might be about arrangements for the weekend or a holiday, or for bigger questions, such as deciding to live together or get married. It might feel hard to risk saying 'no' because you fear falling out while the relationship is being tested. However, saying 'no' to the other person's proposals can actually move the relationship on to the next place. For instance, if your partner asks you to live together or marry them and you say 'no', it opens up the possibility of talking about why. You might have been coasting along for months or years, but at the point they want to commit to you, you can discuss your doubts about them being 'the one', or whether you want to have children together or not. This can enable you both to discuss where you are going in your relationship and what the future holds for you. Sometimes people find that they are actually in two different relationships with each other: perhaps he thinks you're having a 'fling' and you think it's a serious relationship, or vice versa. By saying 'no' to each other's proposals if you are not sure, you will enable the relationship to reveal itself. Of course, I am not suggesting you should say 'no' just as a matter of course in your love relationships - that would be churlish and silly. I am suggesting, however, that you should not be frightened to disagree or even slug things out together.

Urge to merge

It's important that you allow each other space to be separate individuals, with very different desires and agendas. The romantic notion of 'two hearts that beat as one', that many of us swallow and hope for, means couples tend to have the 'urge to merge'. Once they fall in love, have sex, commit, they feel the other person is an extension of themselves, or even a part of themselves, which makes it very hard to say 'no'. Only by discussing things openly, and allowing disagreement, can you really know who you are as individuals within a couple. Always assuming a 'yes', or saying 'yes' when you are not sure or disagree, means you have an unreal relationship. This usually leads to trouble.

I remember being in a restaurant with an ex-boyfriend, for instance, who ordered my meal for me as if I wasn't there. I sat, with my mouth open, about to order the fish, when he ordered, 'Two steaks medium rare'. I was amazed at his audacity, but he simply assumed I would want the same as he was having. He also thought it was 'big' and 'manly' to do so. We hadn't been going out long and didn't know each other well, so it felt awkward as it was our first point of real conflict. I sat for a second, wondering whether to let it go or not, but I was so incensed that I had to say, 'I'm sorry, no, I don't want the steak, I wanted the fish.' He was annoyed and embarrassed and didn't want me to make a fuss, but I decided I would make a fuss on my own behalf. The waiter was fine about it; my then boyfriend wasn't, which is why he became an 'ex'. That incident revealed deeper issues about how he saw me in the relationship - as an extension of himself, rather than a person in my own right. He wanted to merge with me, and I wanted to keep my independence.

Making counterproposals

Being able to say 'no' in an intimate relationship can be helped by making a counterproposal. If your partner suggests going to a new local restaurant but you feel like going to the cinema, you can say, 'It's a great idea, I'd love to, but could we go there next week and see a film tonight?' This kind of counterproposal opens up a new avenue of discussion. You may both say, 'Let's think about it,' and let things sit unresolved for a while as you both think about and process what you want. You don't have to say 'yes' to the first thing the other proposes just to keep the peace. Try and find something you both want.

Listening exercise

This takes just five minutes for each person. Ask your partner or a good friend to try this listening technique. Set a time for five minutes on an alarm. Sit opposite each other, on straight-backed chairs, in a room without distractions (no TV, radio, telephone, children or pets). Take it in turns to listen while the other talks. The rules are: no interruption, no prompting, no discussion, no questions. Just look at the other person, in the eyes, with a warm, relaxed, expectant expression. Just listen. After five minutes swop round, without comment. Afterwards, ask each other how it felt just to be listened to. Make notes in your notebook/computer file. How did it feel to have undivided attention? How often do you have it? Would you like more? We seldom get listened to in this way and it can be very unnerving when we are. This exercise can point up how hard we find it to really listen to others, too.

Making decisions

Couples argue a lot about decisions, joint or sole, especially when those decisions involve money, moving house, having children, changing jobs - in fact, anything to do with Life with a capital L. Change can be frightening, as well as challenging, and exciting, but two people with two different ideas of what life should be often need quite a lot of time to work things out together. For instance, if you or your partner are offered a new job abroad and one of you is settled in your job here, what do you do? How do you make a decision together about something that affects you both so profoundly? Especially if you disagree.

> *Him:* I've been offered a job in Canada for two years. It's a good contract and a great opportunity. I'm really excited about it, it's just what I've been waiting for for ages.

> *You:* Well done, I'm so pleased for you. When do you go?

> *Him:* Not sure, as I've got a three-month notice to work out.

You: (tentatively) I see ... just how will it affect us?

Him: I hadn't thought really, but you could come out for holidays and to visit.

You: Oh, I see. You don't see me coming with you, then?

Him: No, you have your job and life here ... You wouldn't want to, would you?

You: No. I mean, this is a shock to me. But I thought we were going to get married, as we live together. I'm not sure what all this means.

Him: Married? Steady on, we've only been living together a few months, I'm not sure marriage is on the cards.

You: Oh, I see.

Him: (pause) Are you saying you'd throw everything up to come with me if you could?

You: No. Yes. Oh, I don't know. I need to think about it.

Him: Well, if you're not saying 'yes', then you must mean 'no'?

You: No, not necessarily. This is a shock. I need time to think. I don't know what you're offering, if anything.

Him: Neither do I. I need to think. . . *we* need to think, obviously.

This situation can be a very difficult and painful process as you both try to feel your way to an answer. This kind of discussion can end in tears and misunderstanding. Or it might be resolved with time and effort on both parties' parts. What is happening is that both people are trying to work out where they are in the relationship, what they want, what the other wants and where they are going together. It will only work as a process if they try to be as honest as they can be. Fear of rejection, humiliation, being abandoned, can make this kind of discussion flare into a plate-throwing row, or it can even end the relationship altogether if the left-behind partner feels aggrieved. During the above process both partners need to feel they can say 'no' to the other's proposals if they want to. They don't need to be hurtful, but they do need to be straight. Either party only saying what they think the other one wants to hear would lead to confusion and frustration. Without communicating their real feelings they would never be able to get to a yes, either. It could also be a reversed situation, with you being offered a new post in another city or country, and your partner assuming they will follow you - or not, as the case may be. If you don't want them to come with you, you will have to say 'no'. This can enable your relationship to be authentic and to grow organically as something unique to you both. Decisions can flow from you being real with each other and joint projects will work well because you both put your energy into them. It also means you stay true to yourself as an individual and to yourselves as a couple, no matter how awkward it may feel at the time.

Testing your love

Love relationships develop their own shape, nature and ground-rules. What is right for one couple might be wrong for another. The rules of engagement are usually worked out over time, and once a relationship gets serious and a couple are either living together or getting married, ground-rules usually become more specific and meaningful. As couples learn to trust, be intimate, share life and love each other, the stakes get higher as there is more to lose. However, humans being what we are, there will be many situations which will inevitably 'test' the relationship, such as extra-marital affairs, spending too much money, being economical with the truth, gambling, breaking the law, redundancy, wider family pressures, deciding whether to have children or take on step-children or adopt, moving house and so on.

Everyday negotiations

There will also be everyday situations, such as making arrangements, planning a holiday, decorating the house or redesigning the garden, having a party, organising the weekend, going shopping, having friends round, picking up children or going out socialising, which will need to be negotiated. If one of you does something the other one dislikes or hasn't agreed to, then saying 'no', and saying it effectively, will be crucial to your relationship's ongoing success. For instance, one woman I know found her husband on the Internet nightly, looking at porn channels. She told him she didn't like it and wanted him to stop. He agreed but continued regardless, as he was hooked. In the end, when huge bills rolled in, she had to say a very blunt 'no' to him in a way that would deal with his addiction. She threatened to end their relationship if he continued to use the porn. This finally got through to him and, with counselling help, he stopped. Her 'no' was effective, but only because she gave him two or three chances to give it up for himself and also because she would have carried through her threat. Making empty threats never works - you have to mean them to be effective.

Similarly, a man I know found his partner was spending excessively on their joint credit card. She was spending literally thousands on clothes and shoes. She had had a recent miscarriage and was utterly grief-stricken and also angry with her partner, who she felt was not being empathic. Hence she went on a spending spree. She knew that he would be upset and, in a sense, that is why she took revenge by hitting him in his wallet, where he could feel it. He found out and was furious and told her she could no longer spend on their card. She continued spending, until they had a terrible row. He threatened to end the relationship if she didn't stop spending, and she then poured out how his indifference to her miscarriage had made her feel. His 'no' to her spending enabled the relationship to tackle the problem of their miscarriage, and they then went to relationship counselling together to work through the aftermath of their loss.

If your partner or spouse is doing something you don't like, you have every right to say 'no'. Equally, you need to think about the places you say 'yes' when you mean 'no' and feel resentful afterwards.

Renegotiating your relationship

If you have fallen into a certain pattern with each other, it can be quite difficult to change how you behave. If one of you is more dominating, or the other simply expects to get their way, then when the one who would usually appease stands up for themselves fireworks usually fly. This is fine, but may well be uncomfortable for some time hence. Changing a relationship from within takes hard work and honesty. It is possible, but it takes both of you to agree that, indeed, something needs to change. It may be a question of moving two steps forward and one back for a while, but you can eventually get there with some persistence and determination. You need to give it time, and really try to learn to listen to each other, while letting your feelings move through different stages as they are processed psychologically. This is often a point where couples go to a counsellor or therapist to help them renegotiate the ground-rules of their relationship, or even to save it altogether.

Love and the Disease to Please

We saw in Part One of this book that chronic people-pleasers and codependents (see Chapters 2 and 3) can be the ultimate relationship doormats. Long-term relationships can be very difficult and unsatisfying if one of you adopts this posture. Even though we're in the twenty-first century and modern feminist ideas have been around for at least the last forty years, some women can still find themselves thinking and behaving in outdated traditional ways. The pejorative term 'ballbreaker' has often been attached to women who are perceived as being too dominating or strong. This has led some women to play Barbie to Ken, by contorting themselves into being what they think a potential partner wants or needs, rather than being their true selves.

'I want to please my man': Doranna's story

Doranna is a very attractive twenty-seven-year-old whose overbearing husband constantly criticised her appearance and clothes. Dean, twenty-nine, is a bodybuilder and car mechanic, and Doranna works in a gym as a trainer. They don't have children and Doranna works hard to improve her body image, health and fitness. Unfortunately, Doranna looked up to Dean's knowledge about health and appearance too much. 'He told me I was getting fat and should lose a few pounds most of the time,' she explains tearfully. 'If I put on an outfit I liked he'd say, "You're not going out in that, are you?" It really hurt.'

It's hard to understand why an intelligent and attractive woman like Doranna behaved like a doormat, but she usually found herself scuttling off to the bedroom to change into something else. Why? She confesses to having been desperate to please Dean and wanted his love and approval. She adored him and believed she could change his critical stance towards her, if she only tried hard enough. Dean, however, was not to be satisfied. 'No matter what I wore or how I looked, it was never quite right for Dean,' says Doranna wistfully. 'I did so much to please him, but in the end it didn't make a damned bit of difference.' Dean, perhaps inevitably, ran off with a fellow bodybuilder (whose appearance he obviously approved of) who was five years younger than Doranna, wearing, no doubt, the obligatory short skirt to show off her perfectly-honed legs.

At this point, you might be forgiven for thinking 'Thank goodness Dean's gone.' Doranna was devastated, however, as she loved him (or thought she did), although after a few weeks she started dating a young man whom she'd met at her gym. Doranna had not really given herself much time to mourn the passing of Dean. She felt desperate to have a man in her life again as, somehow, dating someone gave her self-esteem a much needed boost. 'I just don't feel attractive if I'm not going out with someone,' she explains. Very soon, Doranna found herself dressing up for her new man in a way she thought would please him. Her attention was drawn all the time to wondering whether he fancied her, whether she was good enough for him and whether she was wearing the right clothes. Of course, Doranna had been deeply hurt by Dean, and her fragile confidence had been smashed. But oddly, even though her new partner never actually commented on her appearance, she started probing him, inappropriately, about her dress sense and her body.

Patterns past their sell-by date

The relationship was only fledgling, but 'When he said he didn't like something I was wearing, I absolutely flipped,' says Doranna. She had not only invited his comments but had actually drawn them out of him, yet she hated what she heard and got very upset as a consequence. Not surprisingly, the affair soon ended. But why on earth did Doranna do this? What was she trying to prove? Doranna had an outdated pattern of wanting to please and appease men, which went back to her unhappy childhood. She had had a very dominating father, who withheld his love. She often had the 'silent treatment' from him if he was angry with her, and she saw him hitting her mother quite regularly. This was obviously terrifying for a small child, even though she had three brothers and two sisters (who were also ignored). The outcome was that she was pretty scared of men in general, and her father in particular. Consequently, in adulthood she was attracted to tough guys, like Dean. However, when she met a man who wasn't brutal (a nice guy, in fact), she actually tried to make him tougher. Why?

Why we re-enact the past

Doranna was in the grip of patterns which were well past their sell-by date. We often do this in life - continue to have ideas and assumptions, and behave in ways, which are well past the time when they were appropriate. Doranna was driven psychologically to make all the men she became intimately involved with into her disapproving, dominating father so that she could re-enact her childhood. Why? She needed to re-enact the past, but in the hope that this time, as a grown up, she would win the battle. Unconsciously, she was trying to heal the past by reliving it in the present. She had never been able to process fully the pain of rejection by her father, or by Dean, so she steamed on into the next love affair and then tried to turn her new man into an oppressor. Her outdated, unprocessed pattern was forcing both of them into traditional roles which had nothing to do with the relationship that might develop if she could only allow it to grow organically. If you, like Doranna, have had a difficult relationship with a parent or parents in the past, or with a family member, teacher or significant adult, it is tempting to keep re-enacting it in adult life, even if it doesn't make you (or others) particularly happy. The hope that the outcome will be different is what drives us to continue repeating these dynamics. It might also be an addictive pull towards creating relationships which are horribly familiar, even if they are really destructive. Doranna was embroiled in an action replay, first with Dean, then with her new man, in the hope that one day they would say, 'Hey, Doranna, you are totally gorgeous. I was wrong, you are right. I love you to the moon and back.' Indeed, she really wanted to hear this from her father, who, of course, was never going to say it. In her dreams. So she projected her feelings about her father on to any relationship she was in at the time. Doranna needed time to mourn and let go of all her failed relationships with men (especially her father), so she could choose a healthy partnership in future.

If you don't let go, you can't say 'no'

Does Doranna's story ring any bells for you? Have you found yourself repeating roles in your relationships, or going to the opposite extreme, in reaction to past pain? If you don't let go, you can't say 'no'. So it's worth spending time not only grieving when relationships end, but trying to understand what went wrong. More importantly, it's vital to understand your role in their decline before you rush off willy-nilly into the next relationship.

Strong boundaries

We all need to be able to say 'no' in our love relationships, otherwise they remain unreal and unbalanced. If you have fallen into a pattern with your partner of appeasing and pleasing, or they have with you, the one who is appeased and pleased will often feel infuriated and frustrated. Plus, they won't respect the doormat partner at all. The truth is nobody loves a doormat. Not really. Even if they make life relatively easy. Nobody wants or needs to get their own way all the time. We all need our partners and lovers to be themselves, to have strong psychological boundaries and to stand their ground.

Male appeasers

One of the ironies of modern life is that men today are often overshadowed by women who are seemingly much stronger than themselves. I know many men who can't say 'no' to their partner and practise avoidance or acquiescence instead. Men can be just as badly afflicted by the Disease to Please, especially if they feel their women are more practically, intellectually or financially competent and/or emotionally sorted out. What does this do to love and sex relationships? Does this make the women happy? Does it satisfy the men? No. Certainly not. The women want their men to be definite, to have an opinion, to be strong, too: not in the old 'macho' pull-you-along-the-floor-by-your-hair kind of way. No, but in the sense of being their true selves. I know many women driven mad because their partners 'don't care' or 'don't know' or 'can't be bothered' to express what they want, so they say 'yes' to keep the peace. The so-called 'new man' has died a death purely because he was not really a man - he was a synthetic, people-pleasing timidy-beasty, trying to be nice. In fact, most women really want men to be real men, with sensitivity *and* strength, but without the bullish bad old ways.

Saying 'no' in sexual relationships

When researching this book I spoke to a woman who told me she had had sex with many men in her youth because she felt sorry for them. She had compromised herself over and over. Deep down she was desperate for love and affection, and she needed validation, too, but at rock bottom she simply felt she couldn't say 'no' to sex. She found herself acquiescing in sexual encounters, although emotionally she didn't want to be there. Only when she met her husband, and fell in love, did she gain the confidence to say 'no' to those she didn't really fancy. Women often find themselves compromised in this way: feeling flattered by a man's attentions, or feeling beholden because he has bought her gifts or a delicious dinner. A woman may flirt, even outrageously; she may engage in kissing and touching, but it doesn't mean she necessarily wants to have sexual intercourse.

I've already mentioned the old feminist adage from the 1970s which goes, 'Whatever we wear, wherever we go, 'yes' means 'yes' and 'no' means 'no'.' This means that, no matter how seductively dressed or naturally attractive a woman is, a man has no right to have sex with her unless it is through mutual consent. It is still true today that sex should always be mutual, something both partners really want. This is true whether you are dating or living together or married. The above also applies to men, who can be forced into unwanted sexual contact, too.

Sexual abuse, sexual harassment, sexual assault and rape

Obviously, the place where 'no' needs to be heeded the most is when one person feels forced into sexual contact by another. Sexual abuse is more common than we like to think in family life, and sexual harassment can happen at work. This means unwanted contact of a sexual nature can happen in private as well as public places, and it can happen to men as well as women. Sexual assault and rape, unfortunately, can happen just about everywhere, often with someone you know and in a love relationship or marriage. In situations where one person is forcing themselves sexually on another, 'no' needs to be loud and clear. However, there are times when screaming 'no' can actually endanger your life (in terms of provoking an attacker to become violent, even to kill). Unfortunately, the law nearly always demands that the victim prove that they resisted, and shouting 'no' or fighting someone off is seen as the biggest proof. In reality, it may be safer to acquiesce quietly and not be injured, or killed, but then go straight to the police with the evidence. This is a sensitive and difficult area of modern life, but has to be mentioned in a book which tackles saying 'no'. It is crucial that you know you have the right to say 'no' to sex, even if you are married or living with someone, and also that they have the right to say 'no' to you. Nobody owns anyone else's body, and mutual respect, dignity and care should be the watchword of any sexual contact. Unfortunately, this is not always the case.

Finally, take a moment to think about your love relationship (if you have one) and your sex life (if you have one). Do you feel you have the right to say 'no'? Are there times you have said or implied 'yes' when you meant 'no'? And are there things you want to bring up with your partner about how sexual matters are between you? Make some notes reminding yourself of any insights you have gained about your love and sex relationships before you move on to the next, equally sensitive, chapter, about saying 'no' to your nearest and dearest.

8

Saying 'no' to family, children and friends

It's a fact of life: the closer someone is to you the harder it can be to say 'no' to them. As in love and sex relationships, it can be very difficult to stand your ground or even work out what you want with intimate family, children and friends. The more entwined you are, the more you love them and feel concerned about their well-being, the more you feel duty-bound and tied emotionally (guilt, anxiety), the harder it can be to be cool and objective. This chapter will look, albeit briefly, at the issues that come up when you need to say 'no' to your nearest and dearest.

Tribal feelings

A family is a tribe, and most of us want to belong to our tribe (think football and the World Cup or any sports, club or community event). Of course, it's only human to want to belong to a specific group - that's how we define ourselves. We have an inherent need to belong, to connect, to interrelate, to depend and to matter to others. Being mutually supportive gives meaning to our lives and ourselves. For instance, one of the most researched subjects on the Internet is genealogy - that is, people finding out about their family histories and names. We want to know who we are, where we come from and where we *belong*. Your family can be your anchor, tethering you safely; but it can also be a ball and chain around your neck.

Breaking family taboos

As much as you want to do the right thing by your family, there will definitely be times when you need to say 'no' or follow an independent path. When you do this, it can feel as if you are breaking a serious cultural taboo, especially in families which are very close-knit, or where there is a lot to lose (this can be down to class, culture, religion, family business, etc.). After all, why do we watch soaps and TV dramas and films so avidly (think *The Sopranos, The Forsyte Saga, Coronation Street, EastEnders, Billy Elliot* or *Last Tango in Halifax).* These microcosmic worlds often telescope our own lives and reflect them back to us: the rivalries, jealousies, life events and emotional undercurrents. Saying 'no' in the face of familial or cultural assumptions is nearly always a major theme: not taking on the family business, coming out as gay, not marrying an 'approved' partner, or becoming an artist, for example. Saying 'no' to your family can be like breaking the biggest taboo of all. Think of all the phrases you know that tell us how important family are, such as 'blood is thicker than water', or 'family first'. Can you think of more?

Duty, obligation and guilt

Duty, obligation and *guilt,* these three little words can make it hard to say 'no' when dealing with your own family. It's easy to get yourself tied up in knots trying to please everyone on the family front. Families — the tribe — have all sorts of assumptions, beliefs and values and expect you to subscribe to them. If you don't, or you want to move away from them as you grow and develop into a mature adult, then there can be conflict. Even so, you will probably have absorbed a lot of 'shoulds', 'oughts' and 'musts' about your family's desires and needs (go back to Part One for more on this). Our duties towards our parents may not be as clear-cut as they were, say, two generations ago, but we nevertheless feel obligated to them. Even though you technically become adult – and therefore independent – at eighteen, it can take many years before you feel emotionally separate from your parents. Today, most people move away from home and live independently, due to increased affluence, sexual freedom, educational choice and job opportunities. Nevertheless, the emotional ties can remain strong with parents and family, even though many of us live in a diaspora - with family members spread all over the place. We may not have aunties and grannies next door, but we still feel a level of duty, and desire, to visit, phone or keep in touch. Even so, this level of contact may not be enough for older people, who often feel neglected. At the same time, we are generally healthier and living longer, so the old assumptions about what later life actually entails have changed. Your older family members may not be just sitting at home knitting and doing the lotto, they may actually be scaling the Himalayas or surfing the Net. Thus, assumptions about duty and obligation can work both ways: you may not be able to visit whenever an elderly relative wants you to and, equally, they may not be available for childcare when you need it.

Why you need to say 'no' to your family of origin

No matter how much you love them or care about them or simply feel obligated to them, you sometimes have to say 'no' to your family of origin. Why? You may:

- disagree with their plans and have other ideas;
- need some distance from them;
- disagree with their values and principles;
- not get on that well;
- have fallen out over something;
- have had some experiences in the family which haven't been resolved or even discussed.

The issues you might want to say 'no' about may be:

- your choice of life partner;

- your career choice (including not joining in the family business);
- choosing to live with someone instead of marrying them;
- having children or not (or adoption, fostering, surrogacy, etc.) - whether married or unmarried;
- being a lone parent;
- where you live and with whom;
- your lifestyle;
- how often you visit each other;
- your sexuality;
- spending high days and holidays together;
- spending money (including inheritance);
- property (buying, maintaining, selling);
- looking after them in old age.

If you have a robust, healthy, mutually loving, mutually interdependent relationship with your family you will be used to saying 'yes' and 'no' when you want and need to. Saying 'no' will probably not be difficult, simply because you can talk to your parents, extended family and siblings and can work things out. If so, skip this chapter and move on. However, for many of us we have at least one or two issues which we feel awkward or difficult saying 'no' about.

Breaking the mould

'All happy families are alike but an unhappy family is unhappy after its own fashion': so begins Tolstoy's brilliantly tragic novel *Anna Karenina*. It's so utterly true, though, as happy families are much more elastic about the shows of fealty, or duty, than unhappy ones. A good example is what happens about significant events in family life, such as the 'rites of passage' (births, deaths, engagements, anniversaries, weddings, naming ceremonies, circumcisions), which stir up strong feelings on the family front in everyone from Tooting to Timbuktu. A happy family will accept that you may be on night duty, or have just had a baby, or may simply have other things to do if you can't or even don't want to come. They will accept you have your own life and, although disappointed not to see you, won't load guilt upon your shoulders. They may even make it easy for you not to come. In an unhappy family, your absence at such a time will be noted and never forgiven, and/or you will be forced or manipulated to attend out of — yes — duty, obligation and guilt.

How to say 'no' to your family

High days and holidays can raise the family temperature, too: Christmas is coming and the relatives are getting restless. Cultural events can hold great expectations in families. Are you coming home for Christmas/Pesach/Ramadan/Thanksgiving this year? Here's a typical fairly unhappy family scenario:

Parent: (Mother probably — a telephone conversation about a month before Christmas) We haven't seen you for ages. We never hear from you and I suppose you won't be coming home this Christmas *again.* I suppose we'll just be left all alone, staring over the cold turkey at each other...

You: (feeling guilty and getting hooked - you had been wanting to go skiing this year with a new partner) Ah yes, I haven't really thought about it yet, I've been so busy. . .

Parent/Mother: Your sister is coming, of course. She never lets us down. She wouldn't dream of it. But it will still be sad, just being the three of us. Not the same as when Granny was alive *(voice wobbles with emotion).*

You: I have to work right up to Christmas...

Parent/Mother: Work, work, work, that's all you ever think about. What about us, your family, don't we count?

How can you ignore us at Christmas? It's only one day a year, after all.

You: (heart-strings being fully tugged at) Look, Mum, I haven't said I'm not coming, it's just that…

Parent/Mother: What, that we're too boring? Not like your smart city friends.

You: No, it's not that…

Parent/Mother: Well, I don't know what I'll tell your father, he'll be heartbroken.

You: I haven't said 'no', have I?

Parent/Mother: Well, you haven't said 'yes', either…

You: (resigning yourself, getting caught on a 'yes' hook) OK, OK, I'll come if it'll make you happy…

Parent/Mother: Oh, that's wonderful, it'll make your father so happy. Could you come Christmas Eve and stay till after Boxing Day?

Gotcha. You haven't been able to explain anything, or negotiate. Instead, the emotional force of the guilt, duty and obligation has got you where the family ties want you. In fact, if you go home under these circumstances, you will probably be grumpy, be late, - drink too much and end up arguing over Scrabble. Far better to work out what you want and approach the negotiation from a position of power. What can work well with this kind of situation is the cracked record technique (see Chapter 6 for more on this), played lovingly but effectively.

Action replay - with you saying 'no' this time:

Parent/Mother: We haven't seen you for ages. We never hear from you and I suppose you won't be coming home this Christmas *again.* I suppose we'll just be left all alone, staring over the cold turkey at each other.

You: (feeling guilty, but using your thought-out strategy of presenting a counterproposal, plus the cracked record technique. You adopt a warm and concerned tone) Mum, lovely to hear from you. No, I won't make it this Christmas and I'm really sorry, but I'd love to invite you out for a pre-Christmas dinner... on me. There's a lovely place I want to take you and Dad to.

Parent/Mother: Oh, I see *(sounds very disappointed).* You know your sister's coming for Christmas and it'll just be the three of us staring over the cold turkey...

You: (interrupting) Mum, I'm sure it won't be like that, you'll have a lovely time with Sophie. I'm inviting her, too, to lunch. She's already agreed. I'd love you both to join us ...

Parent/Mother: (caught off guard) It's not the same as when Granny was alive, and I'm sure your father will be disappointed. *(voice wobbles with emotion).*

You: (sympathetically) Yes, I know it's not the same without Granny, we all miss her, and I'm sorry Dad will be disappointed, but I have to work up until Christmas ...

Parent/Mother: Work, work, work that's all you ever think about. What about us, your family, don't we count? How can you ignore us at Christmas? It's only one day a year, after all. . .

You: (wobbling a bit at this heart-string tugging, but staying on track) Mum, I know it's difficult, but I really enjoy my job and you're glad I was able to buy my own flat, aren't you? I'm not ignoring you because I'm asking you both out for a lovely Christmas meal. I really want to see you at Christmas, which is why I'm inviting you. Please come. Take some time to think it over, talk to Dad, the offer's there...

In this action replay, you stay on track, you keep calm, you convey warmth in your tone, but you are not guilt-tripped. In order to do this, you need to have thought about what you want ahead of time, and to have dealt with the emotions to some extent by talking to a friend or partner, or dealing with it in therapy or counselling. In time, this kind of negotiation can become second nature and you will no longer be at the mercy of familial duty, obligation and guilt. You have to adopt the attitude and posture of a grown up in this kind of situation, too.

Becoming a grown up

This kind of scenario arises when we are unable to separate emotionally from our families. It can work both ways, from adult children towards their parents, and from parents towards their adult children. Whatever your relationship with your parents is like, the most important aspects of growing up are:

- learning to be separate, adult, responsible for yourself and your own life;
- understanding where the psychological boundaries lie between your own parents and yourself;
- negotiating an ongoing relationship with them that suits you both, once you are fully independent;
- responding to what they need and want in later life, but without sacrificing yourself and your family at the same time.

Tough love

We need to use 'tough love' techniques to create boundaries where there are none, to protect ourselves from being psychologically worn out, and to help both sides of the family regroup once a child has flown the coop. You have to learn to do this with your own parents, and your parents have to learn to do this with you, otherwise you will never grow up emotionally. If you have children, you also have to learn to do it with them - for both your own and their sakes. Mandy's story below is a good example of learning to use 'tough love' to say 'no'.

Mandy's story: learning how to say 'no' to her kids

Mandy, forty-two, has five children ranging from twenty-one to twelve, and was married for twelve years. She works full-time as a store manager. Mandy appeared in the *Woman* magazine article I wrote about women who can't say 'no'. Mandy had been through an acrimonious divorce ten years previously, although her husband still stays in touch with the children. However, life has been very hard, bringing up five children on a single income as a lone parent on a tough housing estate. Mandy admits she felt guilty about the divorce, which led to her becoming 'a permanent doormat'. Stressed, exhausted, emotionally burnt out, Mandy allowed the kids to walk all over her. 'I used to be in the bath, lying there having a lovely soak, and my eldest would come up the stairs and say, "I hope you're not in the bath, I want to get in it, I'm going out," and I'd get straight out.' Mandy became tyrannised in her own home: 'I'd lend them money all the time, they'd use my mobile, I'd be a taxi service running them everywhere, and I used to be a cafe making five different dinners because they were that fussy. It would drive me absolutely nuts to pacify each one.' Although her two eldest children were working adults, they contributed no money to the house and they avoided household chores. 'I was their skivvy,' says Mandy frankly.

Why did she do it all? 'I felt guilty about them not having two parents and I tried to overcompensate. I tried to be both parents, but I failed.' Mandy actually felt scared of her kids, as a couple got in trouble with the law, and felt she couldn't say 'no' to them at all. The crunch came two years ago with the death of her mother, who supported her emotionally and sometimes helped out with the kids, and also the kids ran up an £800 phone bill which Mandy had to pay off. 'That was it,' she says firmly, 'I decided things had to change.' Luckily a support group was being set up through her local authority's Education Department: TULIP (Together United Living In Peace) enabled mums on the estate to talk about their personal struggles and learn some assertiveness skills to say 'no' to their nearest and dearest.

'I learned on the course to say "NO", to turn round and say, "No, I'm not going there or doing that." They'd worn me down, into the ground. A mum's job is hard enough, let alone working.' Mandy changed her whole attitude towards her children. She learned to employ 'tough love' — no more loans, use of her phone or a 24-hour taxi service, and they had to do their bit at home. Mandy now makes sure she goes out once or twice a week, and employs one of the eldest to babysit the others. 'I've gained in confidence and I can stand my ground more. I'll argue now, whereas I wouldn't have before. I tell them, "You're a guest in my house. If you want to stay here, you abide by my rules." It's been hard to turn things around, but Mandy thinks she's winning and TULIP now runs groups for other local mothers who find it hard to say 'no'. 'You need to sit and tell your child why you are saying "no",' says Mandy. 'It doesn't do them or you any good to be a doormat. I say to them, "The answer is NO. What is it you don't understand about the word NO, is it the N or the O?"' With support and some tough emotional work, Mandy has established some firm boundaries; she is using 'tough love' and she has stopped being used and abused. Every time TULIP appears in the national press, they are inundated with letters from mums unable to say 'no'. The need is there. 'My next step is to train as a counsellor so I can really help other mums like me,' Mandy says.

Learning to argue

Learning to argue and stand your ground, like Mandy, is a crucial part of learning to say 'no'. We are often scared to fight with our nearest and dearest because we fear they will stop loving or leave us. But in fact it can be very healthy to have a good row and 'clear the air'. If you have been a doormat in the relationship it is highly likely that you will argue more as you begin to stand your ground. The other person will find it hard that you are standing up to them. Probably, however, they will also feel secretly relieved and they will respect you more for giving up your doormat stance. Close relationships can usually live through this kind of transition, if there is enough love and goodwill to keep them afloat. People often say they are nastiest with their nearest and dearest and, indeed, many of us test out those closest to us, to see if they will stick with us, regardless of how we behave. This can lead to people being abused, in extreme cases, but if someone who has become a doormat, like Mandy, begins to stand up for themselves, the dynamic can change completely — for the better.

The Disease to Please and saying 'no' to family

It can be doubly difficult to say 'no' to family members if you are also drowning in the Disease to Please. Women, in particular, can find themselves running around trying to please and appease everyone, as we have seen earlier. Codependent women, who wrap themselves round addicted and emotionally absent partners/spouses trying to 'save' or 'control' them, can almost destroy themselves in their fruitless quest for perfection and sainthood. Jilly Shaul, a sixty-four-year-old life coach who has been married for over forty years with four grown-up children, told me candidly that in her generation there were few choices available to women. 'My mother thought I was on the shelf by twenty-two, so when I met my husband she told me I was to ease his path the whole time. As a consequence, I looked up to him, hero-worshipped him and tried hard to fulfil the role that I had seen my mother fulfil - conditioning, really.' Jilly became a devoted, exhaustively hardworking, traditional wife and mother. 'I have spent all of my life (until recently) pleasing all the family. I did everything for ten years without a day off and eased the path for everyone but me.' Jilly, like many women of her generation, felt duty bound to nurture her own parents in old age, a task she took on unflinchingly. It was only when she reached her forties that she panicked about her own life. 'I'd been so accommodating. I'd never had time off, my husband had never changed a nappy or cooked a meal, and I'd looked after my parents, my kids, my husband, when suddenly I thought, "What's happened to my own life?"'

Jilly managed to find herself an administrative job — which she did for free, as she was so desperate to learn some skills, gain some experience and get out of the house once the children were independent. Now, twenty years later, she is a successful businesswoman in her own right, running her own life-coaching business, helping other women to say 'no' to family demands in order to get their own lives on track. She's still a devoted mother and wife, but she has set some firm boundaries and takes time out for herself.

Understandably, Jilly's relationship went through a lot of turmoil once she decided to 'get a life'. It was a sort of Shirley Valentine moment, with her giving up being a domestic drudge and doormat to find herself. Her husband was not happy with the transitional period, although she says he (grudgingly) accepts it now. Nevertheless, they have stayed together through it all. Again, Jilly had to employ her intelligence, her people skills and 'tough love' to get what she wanted. 'I don't like confrontation, but I have learned to stand my ground. This has brought me happiness, independence and a sense of self, albeit late in life. Most of all, I'm pleasing myself, at last.'

Saying 'no' to friends

It can be just as hard to say 'no' to friends as it is to family members, as we saw in Part One of this book. Friendship is a very important part of life and, of course, we develop friendships at different levels of intensity and of different types throughout our lives. Typically, adolescents (especially girls) can develop extremely passionate and entangled friendships, in which it is hard to say 'no'. Look at any pair of teenage girls and they will usually be dressed identically, like clones, which means if one of them dissents there is usually trouble. This pattern can continue throughout women's lives, with them pairing off based on what they have in common. This means they often fall out if one changes her lifestyle or opinions. Saying 'no' can feel like a threat to the relationship - although it isn't, it's actually an assertion of independence.

People from unhappy families often invest a great deal in friends as an alternative to family life. Some people actually build a substitute family out of friends. These friendships are important and can get very complex emotionally, as some people look for a replacement father or mother figure or siblings in their best friend. The same heated emotions concerning abandonment, love, respect, guilt and anxiety can occur, and people can form friendships and 'split up' just like any love relationship. As with sexual relationships and family matters, it is important to try and have firm boundaries with friends. The more desperate you are to be liked and accepted, to belong to a particular tribe (like a gang), the less it will probably work. If you get led into all sorts of situations and activities (such as joining in heavy drug or drinking sessions) because you can't say 'no' to a mate, this can make you open to abuse in the friendship.

You then have to question whether it is a friendship at all, or whether you are just a doormat.

It can be tricky to refuse a friend's request for something, because you want to 'prove' that you are best mates, or you are tough, or you care. Susie, a beauty therapist, told me her best mate always borrows money from her to buy expensive clothes, which she pays back over weeks. 'My friend doesn't trust herself with a credit card, so she uses me like a bank,' she said. Recently, her friend wanted to buy an £800 Versace suit for a wedding and Susie, who was saving for her holidays, had to say 'no'. 'I was amazed,' says Susie, 'my mate absolutely went ballistic and I realised she'd seen me as a soft touch. I told her straight she could go and use her own credit card and stop using me.' They fell out. Susie now questions what, exactly, the friendship was about. By saying 'no' she learned something about how she was valued in the friendship. Had the friendship had more to it than her being a useful money-lending doormat, then her friend would have apologised and made reparations. So saying 'no' can help you work out exactly what the strengths and weaknesses of your friendship are.

Setting limits

I remember a friend (actually she was more of an acquaintance) arriving from Germany to stay with me for one night. She wasn't a close friend and I was taking her in at the last minute because she was stranded. She stayed the first night, which was fine, and then simply settled in for a whole week. Every day I thought, 'How can I tell her to go?' as we munched my muesli together. I felt irritated as I was feeling put upon. She was disturbing my work, as I work from home, and she didn't go out and buy bread and milk or offer to contribute to the household costs (there is an art of being a good guest). I realised, by day three, that she felt she had found a friendly nest and would simply stay for the duration of her two-week holiday. She was banking on me not saying 'no' to her. She didn't ask me if she could stay longer and I simply felt embarrassed to bring up the subject. How on earth do you say, 'I want you to go,' and stay friends or be polite? It felt impossible, but I moaned to my friends about how used I was feeling. I began to count every slice of bread she happily consumed with my butter and jam. Eventually, driven to distraction by her draping herself on my sofa and helping herself to my wine, I found the courage to say, 'It's been lovely to have you stay, but I really need you to leave soon. Can you go tomorrow?' She looked affronted, as she had been banking on me not setting limits — she wanted to sponge off me as long as she could. 'Can't I stay another night?' she said, pouting. I simply said 'no', I was sorry but that wouldn't be convenient. She was, after all, only an acquaintance, and she was, in fact, the one behaving badly. I felt terribly guilty, but also angry that she had made me feel responsible for her. Somehow I had got hooked into saying 'yes', even a silent one, because I felt so rude to say 'no'. Yet she was the one actually taking advantage of me. As she left next day she was actually quite cheerful about going. I later discovered that she had gone to stay with another friend of a friend for the last week of her holiday. People like that depend on finding doormats to step on. However, doormats play their part in being passively stepped upon.

I learned a somewhat painful lesson from this experience. Even with friends, it is important to set limits and to have boundaries. It wasn't that she had a problem (although her attitude was questionable), it was me who couldn't set a limit with her. So many unspoken assumptions can lurk under the surface between people that wires can get crossed if you are not straight with each other. You might feel you don't need to articulate things with friends, but you do. It can seem excruciatingly hard to turn a friend down - what are friends for, after all, if not to help each other? But you do have to - when it's not right for you. You have to be able to say 'no', even disappoint and let them down, otherwise you can get into a real pickle with each other.

Healthy relationships are based on mutual, respectful care and thoughtfulness, but this doesn't mean agreeing with or to everything the other person suggests. For instance, your friends want you to take their kids for the weekend so they can go away. You want to help them, but you really don't want to do it this weekend. So you have to say 'no'. If you say 'yes' in these circumstances it will simply all go wrong, because you will do a favour for the wrong motives. The more confident you are, the more you will be able to say 'no' to someone very close to you and risk falling out. In family life it is essential for children to see their parents disagreeing and then resolving their conflicts. It is unhealthy either to suppress all conflict (it's like living in poison gas) or to be at war all the time. Similarly, children make friendships where they play out roles they see in their family, so the more they are able to experience the cut and thrust of saying 'no' and resolving differences in family life, the more they will be able to disagree with friends, learn to stand their ground, and even fight their corner, while still being able to continue relating.

Love and sex relationships, family, children and friends are obviously the closest relationships we have. However, many of us spend most of our waking lives with strangers, at work, and we also come into contact with all sorts of people in authority (such as doctors, teachers, the police) and even people who try to attack us on the street. It is to this last, everyday experience of needing to say 'no' that we now turn.

9

Saying 'no' at work, to authority and in public places

It can be hard to say 'no' at work because most of us want to keep our jobs and please our boss. It's also important to be a good workmate or colleague and, of course, keep the customer/client happy if we work closely with people. Work is a crucial part of life and we do it for a number of reasons. Obviously, most of us need to earn money to live and that is our primary motive for working. However, there is an inherent psychological need to be involved in meaningful activity; work can be creative and more than a means to an end. For some it can be a vocation, a career, the centre of life. For others, it is simply a way of getting money to pay the bills and mortgage/rent.

Work also has tribal aspects, in that it brings you into contact with an organisation or group, so there is a sense of belonging, similar to belonging to a family (see Chapter 8 for more on this). Strong feelings can become attached to work and the workplace, and what it represents to you psychologically. People gain status, power, achievement and a sense of self-worth from working. Think of what happens when we meet someone at a party - what's the first question we usually ask? 'What do you do for a living?' We form a picture of the kind of person they are as to whether they answer 'vet' or 'road sweeper'. So what you do signals to people (rightly or wrongly) what kind of personality and lifestyle you probably have.

Similarly, because we spend so much time at work (we often see more of our colleagues than our own families or children), work relationships can become pretty crucial in our lives. We often 'project' feelings from our family backgrounds on to our bosses and colleagues. For instance, the bad-tempered female boss can remind you, albeit unconsciously, of your bad-tempered mother, or your competitive colleague can remind you of your competitive brother or sister. Because of this, deeply unconscious feelings are sometimes stirred up at work: rivalry, envy, jealousy, anger, resentment, and these can colour how you feel about doing your job and the people you have to deal and work with: these unresolved feelings can also make you say 'yes' automatically, when you want to say 'no'.

People-pleasing and work

If you are a people-pleaser, you might well find that you are pulling yourself in a million directions at once, trying to be 'nice' and accommodating, a model worker in the 'Happy Helper' mode, in the hope your boss will notice or your colleagues will like you, or you'll get that promotion or bonus if you go that extra mile. Unfortunately, this can often backfire on you as a strategy, because the doormat at work usually remains just that, a downtrodden doormat. It's the pushy, assertive strategists who can say 'no' and who have strong psychological boundaries, *and* who can get the job done, who are usually rewarded with good pay, promotion and perks. I heard a fascinating speech by a top male editor of a daily tabloid newspaper recently. He explained to the (largely female) audience the difference between how male reporters and female reporters negotiated their pay deals (in his experience). The women would enter his office, somewhat gingerly, and put their case for a 'reasonable' pay rise. He found they could be negotiated down quite easily and were often simply grateful to be keeping their jobs or getting a small promotion. The men, on the other hand, would waltz in, ask for an astronomical increase plus a flash car and other perks, and then threaten to walk if they didn't get it. Who got what they wanted? Both, usually. Although, of course, the men got more because they simply asked for and expected more. The men simply said 'no' to the editor's first offer, because they had the confidence (arrogance? brassneck?) to be able to turn it down, whereas the women, conditioned to appease and ask for less, largely accepted the first offer they were made. They simply didn't risk saying 'no'. This might seem horribly stereotypical, but it indicates that men (or at least a certain type of man) will be able to say 'no' more comfortably than many women, who are much more focused on people-pleasing and conforming to the status quo. If you are a people-pleaser, you are going to have to think outside the box and start taking risks to move on in your life (if you want to).

Saying 'no' at work

Many people I spoke to about this book said they felt it was harder than ever to say 'no' at work today. Job insecurity, the rise of short-term contracts and self-employment, along with our stressful lifestyles, means that it can be hard not only to turn work down but also to negotiate the terms that you really want. The Americanisation of our work culture (the 24/7 lifestyle), along with the decrease in unionisation and decline in welfare rights, means that people often feel they have to accept whatever is on offer at work. One woman, working in the IT industry, told me her bosses just kept unilaterally upping the hours she had to work. She was expected to work long days, well into the evening, to take work home, and usually work weekends. She was also supposed to be ready to travel to any destination at a moment's notice. When she said 'no' to yet another weekend away (she had a family wedding to go to) she was told she was not committed enough to the job and summarily sacked. With hindsight, she realised she should have put her foot down much earlier, but she had felt she should conform to the largely male work ethos of the company. Luckily, by the time she was able to say 'no' she had already worked out a strategy to take her career forward by setting up her own business, so she was able to take a risk.

So what do you need in order to say 'no' at work?

- **self-confidence and self-worth**: this needs building;
- **a sense of the rightness of your cause:** you won't win an argument or a battle if you are not doing your job properly;
- **courage:** ability to walk away from the job;
- **knowledge**: prepare your ground, do your homework;
- **support:** union, colleagues, friends, family, partner;
- **strategy**: work out what you want and how you are going to get it;
- **integrity:** you need to be trustworthy, honest and able to produce the goods. Don't gossip or put others down - it usually backfires;
- **tenacity and determination:** if at first you don't succeed, approach the problem from another angle and keep going;
- **emotional intelligence**: don't be belligerent, have the wit to know how to handle your own and others' feelings;
- **psychological boundaries**: best to keep your private life private, your work life at work. Be careful about mixing the two, it often doesn't work.

How to say 'no' at work

Whether you are an employer, an employee or self-employed, you will need to be able to say 'no' effectively to all sorts of people at work. If you find yourself saying 'yes' when you mean 'no', or you are feeling stressed out because you have become a doormat, try thinking about the following basic tips for work success:

- **Do your job and do it well:** meet deadlines, be accurate, don't agree to what you can't achieve.
- **Treat people appropriately:** don't look for love, approval, affection from your boss, colleagues or employees. Keep your relationship appropriate to work—it will be easier to be professional and to say 'no' when you need to.

- **Improve your performance:** take time to think about how you do your job well and how to improve your performance.
- **Buy time:** if you are asked to do something on top of your already stacked work load, say, 'Could you give me five minutes/until the end of the day/until tomorrow to think about it and I'll get back to you?' Take time out to look at your work load realistically and think about how you can achieve your current and future goals.
- **Negotiate:** you don't have to accept the first thing you are offered, but you do have to be prepared to negotiate. Be prepared to say 'no' calmly, politely, firmly, perhaps with a diplomatic smile, and only say 'yes' when you have negotiated what you want.
- **Learn to confront:** sometimes you will have to say 'no' to someone breaking company rules, or mistreating you in some way at work. Maybe you'll have to fight your corner or sack someone. You will have to learn to say, 'No, that is not acceptable,' to all sorts of things. Don't be afraid to confront the situation if you need to. If you don't, you will be a 'yes' man or woman and will become a workplace doormat. You certainly won't survive self-employment if you can't confront people.
- **Take risks:** not silly ones, but you do need to be prepared to take a risk if you want to say 'no'. Sometimes it will work, sometimes not. Whatever, you will learn something about yourself and new opportunities may open up.

Saying 'no' to authority

Apart from being able to say 'no' to your boss effectively and negotiate what you want, there are plenty of other situations in life where you need to be able to. say 'no' to people in authority. It is important to be able to deal effectively with people in authority like police officers, traffic wardens, bank managers, bureaucrats, utility providers (like gas, electricity, etc.), teachers, salespeople, your MP and, of course, medical and all sorts of other professionals. We can feel overawed by authority because we felt powerless at home or school, or were bullied or are physically small or emotionally fragile. It is possible to overcome this kind of experience or tendency by learning some basic assertiveness skills, with or without some counselling help.

'Trust me, I'm a doctor'

Medical professionals are typical authority figures and many of us find them quite hard to deal with, especially the higher up the medical hierarchy you go. For instance, nurses and midwives might be very friendly and helpful, but doctors and hospital consultants can be quite intimidating. You know you've usually got about five minutes' consultation time with them and they are always busy and distracted, often exhausted. It's obviously a broad generalization – bedside manners have improved and there is the 'Patient's Charter' – but you know that you are mainly a 'leg' or 'heart' to them, not a person, and they usually have a brusque air of 'trust me, I'm a doctor - don't ask any questions' written all over them. It can seem difficult to stand up to someone who has your health in their hands, as you may fear if you are perceived as 'trouble' they may refuse prescribing a drug you need or, worse, saw the wrong leg off as a consequence. Doctors certainly don't like it very much, in my experience, if you either ask too many questions (it takes up valuable time) or refuse their treatment altogether. This is not an attack on doctors - although they are particular figures of authority many people find it hard to say 'no' to, doctors do a tremendous job generally, under tremendous pressure and with minimal resources. Nonetheless, you may want to say 'no' to a certain course of action or treatment and it can feel pretty difficult to do so.

Here's a typical scenario that you might encounter in your GP's surgery. You've had two minutes to explain a recurring medical problem and the doctor has only glanced up at you briefly.

Doc: (not looking at you, typing the prescription on the computer) Right, I'm prescribing you a week's course of steroids, which should clear the trouble up. Take one twice a day after eating, and complete the course.

You: Yes, fine ... er... I...

Doc: OK? Good, good. Come back and see me if it doesn't clear up.

You: Ah, I, er... *(wanting to ask questions, but intimidated as GP indicates the door).*

Doc: Goodbye. Next...

If you had prepared your case and thought about what you wanted (you can write a list of questions down before you go into the doctor's surgery) the consultation could have been very different.

Action replay:

Doc: (not looking at you, typing the prescription on the computer) Right, I'm prescribing you a week's course of steroids, which should clear the trouble up. Take one twice a day after eating, and complete the course.

You: (summoning up your courage) Thank you, Doctor. Just one question. Are there side-effects?

Doc: (still not looking up) Well, there might be, very occasionally, but I usually find they are fine with patients.

You: (persisting) I read you can get palpitations and swelling of the joints, and I have to say I'm not happy to take steroids.

Doc: (looking at you for the first time, a bit irritated at your home diagnosis) Oh?

You: (continuing a bit more confidently, even though you feel a bit awkward) Yes. I would really appreciate it if you could offer an alternative treatment.

Doc: (annoyed, but resigned) Oh, I see. Well, there is an alternative... *(flicking through prescribing book)* Um, it's not a steroid, so it may not work as well... or even at all...

You: Could I try it?

Doc: Um, well... I don't see why not. You could take it for a week and come back if it doesn't do the trick.

You: (much relieved not to be taking a steroid, for now, at least) Thank you, Doctor, it's very much appreciated. I'll obviously come back if it doesn't work. I'm very grateful to you for finding me an alternative.

This is a very different scenario from the first one because you have taken back some power in the situation. You will often find that people in authority have been trained to deal with the public in a blanket kind of way, so if you handle them politely but firmly, while standing your ground, you may well get a far better result than you originally anticipated. They will begin to see you as an individual, as you are rewriting the script. To some extent we create our own outcomes. Approach a figure of authority powerlessly and they will be all-powerful. Approach them with confidence, charm, humour, information, courtesy (they like their superior knowledge to be acknowledged) but with a counterproposal or plan, and, who knows, they may well respond to you as a unique human being. It's well worth a try, whether you are looking for an extension to your overdraft or house, or whether you want to be upgraded on an aeroplane from standard to business class.

To summarise, if you need to stand up to someone in authority, it is a good idea to:

- **prepare your case**: do your homework/research and work out what it is you want. Make sure you get your facts right, with paperwork back-up, if you want to argue your case;
- **stay calm**: don't lose your temper or be rude. Speaking in calm, clear tones will work wonders. Only get 'angry' in a controlled way, when you want to make an impact;
- **charm:** it may seem strange, but personal charm can go a long way in getting you what you want with authority. I don't mean show off your fishnet stockings to a traffic warden who is booking your car, but being irresistible, witty, charming can get you out of all sorts of sticky situations. A good book to read on this is Philippa Davies' *Irresistibility: Secrets of Selling Yourself* (Hodder & Stoughton, 2000);
- **never threaten:** you could end up in real trouble and without getting what you want. If you threaten sanctions or give an ultimatum, you must see it through, otherwise it is meaningless;
- **be polite:** don't swear at someone in authority, no matter how riled you might be. Staying polite is a powerful tool in getting what you want;
- **buy time:** 'Can I think about it and come back tomorrow/ next week or phone or email you?';
- **use the techniques** found in Chapter 6, such as the sandwich technique: 'I appreciate your help, but I don't want to take steroids. Could you suggest another course of action? I appreciate you thinking about my case more widely,' etc.

Saying 'no' in public places

It can be easier to say 'no' in a public place to something you don't want, because it is the least intimate situation of all. You might find, even if you can't say 'no' to your mum or granny, that you can say 'no' to a person approaching you with a clipboard on the street. You are busy, late for work or have kids trailing, and you say a crisp 'No, thank you, not today'. However, there are situations where saying 'no' might feel difficult to handle in public. This is especially when you feel embarrassed or under the spotlight: in a restaurant, at a counter being served, in the bank or in a queue, for instance. If someone is trying to sell you something you don't want on the street, including drugs, you might simply turn round and walk in the opposite direction. But if you are brought a meal you didn't order in a trendy restaurant, you might find it much harder to turn it down and send it back, even though you are paying. Of course, it is possible and often necessary to say 'no' in public, although a lot of people find themselves saying 'yes' because they don't want to 'make a fuss' or attract attention to themselves unduly. If you have to say 'no' to something, then you need to employ a similar strategy to saying 'no' to authority. You need to be firm, calm, polite, but stand your ground. Simply shouting or being rude seldom gets you what you want (you'll probably be ignored or, worse, bundled out by 'heavies', even arrested).

Handling being attacked

I was once on a train, alone in an empty carriage, deep in a book, when I was accosted by a man demanding my wallet. Oddly, I had just been to an assertiveness workshop as part of my counselling training and, although I was all alone in the carriage, I simply said 'no' quietly and confidently to his demand. He looked at me in astonishment and repeated, 'Give me your wallet' (he was standing over me at the time). Without thinking, I looked up, smiled sweetly and simply said a calm, firm and polite 'no'. To my utter surprise he sat down next to me and said, 'So you're not going to give me your wallet then?' to which I said, 'No.' 'OK, then,' he said, simply, and he sat next to me in silence and got off at the next stop. Only once he'd left the train did I start shaking. I thought, 'What on earth was I doing? He could have pulled a knife on me - why did I say 'no'?' Now, I'm not advocating for a moment that you do the same. In fact, I'm sure the police would advise that you hand your money, mobile or whatever straight over, as it is far better than losing your life. But I guess because I had been to an assertiveness training workshop I had built up my confidence and had worked a lot on my fear, and was feeling unusually centered, calm and confident. I think I must have exuded power and made the man feel he simply could not win. It was a battle between our psyches, rather than anything else. I was polite, friendly, but definite. 'No,' I said, unflinchingly, 'you can't have it.' I wasn't confrontational and I wasn't afraid, I was just matter-of-fact. So imagine my amazement when he simply gave up trying and left me alone. Even more amazingly, I wrote an article for a women's magazine the next day describing my experience, so I actually earned my living by turning something bad to good (a kind of modern-life alchemy). My point here is: you do not have to be a victim, but you do have to be smart. If you can build your confidence and self-esteem, then there are many more choices open to you in terms of how you behave in your life. If you have opened your mouth and said 'yes' more times than you can bear (and kicked yourself afterwards) then the time has come to risk saying 'no'. I'm not urging you to risk your life - please don't - but I am urging you to decide to become your true self. It is to this theme that we now turn, in the final part of this book.

Part Four

Becoming Your True Self

10

Living free of the Disease to Please

Choosing when to say 'yes'

The telephone rang one bright sunny morning recently and I was offered some interesting work which was very poorly paid and didn't really suit my schedule. The work would have been quite demanding and I would have ended up almost paying to do the job. I opened my mouth to say 'yes', absolutely on automatic. After all, one of the credos of self-employed life is that you say yes to everything, every time, everywhere. My mouth stayed open, but I paused. I don't know why. Somewhere, deep in the back of my mind, I heard a little voice saying, 'Don't take it, you don't want it, it will only be trouble, it's not worth it, turn it down.' Suddenly, out of my mouth I heard a voice say, 'Thank you very much for offering me the job, but I won't be able to do this one. It's not enough money, I'm afraid, although I would love to do it. Come back to me if I can help in the future in any way with other projects.' It was a very amicable phone call and I skipped round my office afterwards feeling utterly liberated.

What was the outcome? The company phoned back an hour later and offered me double the money to do the job. I thanked them graciously and still found myself saying, 'I'll think about it,' buying myself an hour's thinking time. I asked myself, once off the phone, do I want to do this job, is the pay enough for the trouble involved? I found myself thinking, on balance, yes, that I would do it. I rang back and the deal was struck. What a wonderfully rich, emancipating experience it was to be in the position of choosing. I had been under the cosh of the Disease to Please for so long that I believed I had to say 'yes' automatically to everything in order to succeed and survive. What I learned on that bright sunny morning was that if you really sound confident and successful, if you have the courage to turn things down or suggest other terms and say 'no', and you handle people well, you might even find things work out better for you. I found that I could choose to say 'yes'. I didn't have to be an automaton. I also learned that 'no' could be a very powerful word, if said in the right way. I went up in the estimation of the company involved because I was felt to be powerful (after all, only people with lots of work can turn work down). I also went up in my own estimation, because I felt I had exercised some choice over my life.

Take a moment to think about your own life. Where would you like to feel you could say, 'I'll think about it'? What would it be like for you not to say 'yes' automatically, and to whom? What would have to change in your attitude and behaviour? In Chapter 1, we met the Four 'Yes' Hooks: in other words, the four main emotional reasons which can lead us into saying 'yes' instead of 'no'.

The Four 'Yes' Hooks are:

1 You want to be NICE.
2 You want to be LIKED/LOVED/RESPECTED.
3 You FEAR LOSING friends, lovers, family, work and social position, success, money, material goods.
4 You feel you DONT HAVE THE RIGHT TO SAY 'NO'.

In order to get yourself off the Four 'Yes' Hooks you would need, therefore, to adopt a new attitude, as follows:

1 **not be nice** (at least not all the time, and not fear not being nice);
2 **not care if people didn't like, love or respect you** (at least not care if everyone didn't — you'd be more choosy about whose opinion really mattered);

3 **not fear losing people or things if you said 'no'** (you'd have the confidence to expect someone or something else to come along);

4 **feel you had the right to say 'no'** if you wanted to.

Seven steps to freedom of choice

Step 1 towards curing the Disease to Please is to take the above four points seriously and to heart. If you do, your self-esteem will grow, your self-worth will blossom. You will be in a position of choosing, which is extremely empowering and liberating.

Believe me, I know.

In fact, you are in a position of choosing what you do with your life, and if you want to cure the Disease to Please you will have to start right now, by choosing to give up saying 'yes' automatically. You will need to take risks and learn to buy time to think, in order to learn to say 'no'.

Choosing when to help

The Happy Helper Habit, which we met also in Chapter 1, can make you seem like one of those people you find working in a fast-food restaurant wearing a smiley-face badge which boasts 'happy to help'. Of course, they are, they are trained to be. That's what they are paid for. However, underneath the smiley masks the people are still people, full of complex feelings, good and bad moods, and are as mixed up as the rest of us. Nobody can be that happy and helpful all of the time (you should listen to what they say in the back rooms of the restaurant). But you, in your life, you are not here to be a Happy Helper to everyone. That is not your sole role in life, and even if it seems it is, your life will be fairly poor in quality and content if you live for collecting your spiritual Brownie points. I am not saying don't be a loving daughter or son, or a caring husband or parent, or a good neighbour or citizen. I am saying that every human being has their own needs, and to deny your own is to deny that you are human. You can help others, of course you can, as long as it is healthy caring, with strong emotional boundaries, and therefore something you do as a *real choice*. Otherwise, you are at risk of being an empty Happy Helper, and even a codependent person, who has very unhealthy, addictive relationships based on guilt and control (see Chapter 3 for more on this). Step 2 towards living free of the Disease to Please is: you need to be able to *choose* to help. How can you do this?

- **Resign, right now, from Compulsive Carers Corp.** Your life membership is terminated, the corporation has gone bust - it wasn't really working in the state it was in.
- **Acknowledge you have your own needs and wants** - put attention on sorting out your own life.
- **Wait until people ask you for help** — stop jumping in and interfering, or obsessing about other people's lives and problems. Give people the chance to come towards you when they are ready and be prepared for them not to approach you at all.
- **Stop being a saviour, a saint, a martyr.** Nobody really likes people like this; it makes them feel uncomfortable, awkward and beholden.
- **Give other people around you more responsibility to help - not only themselves, but others.** You'll be surprised how many other helping hands are around, if you let them have a go. They may do things differently than you would, but others are usually there to help — if you let them.
- **Learn to ask for help yourself when you need it.** If you always seem self-sufficient you can't really have mutually satisfying relationships with people. A bit of genuine give and take never goes amiss.
- **Weed out dead-end relationships.** If you are letting yourself be drained by friendships or relationships past their sell-by date, give them up. Why continue?

Building your self-confidence

The best cure for the Disease to Please is step 3: building your self-confidence. It won't happen overnight, but it will happen if you decide to do the following:

- **Accept yourself:** you are who you are. You need to accept that you are who you are and that it is absolutely fine. An enormous amount of time, energy, effort and anxiety goes into *not* accepting ourselves in terms of physical appearance (body, height, weight, hair and skin colour) and personality. You can do a lot to maximise your natural physical qualities and you can do a great deal to get the best out of yourself. However, the first crucial step has to be: accept yourself as you are. Paradoxically, only then can things actually change for the better.
- **Try this exercise:** look in the mirror and instead of being critical of your looks and body, notice five things you like. Note them down. There will be parts of your appearance which please you. Then note down five aspects of your personality you like (for instance, you are warm, thoughtful, fun, etc.). Stick these ten good attributes on your bathroom mirror on a Post-It note and remind yourself every time negative thoughts come into your mind about yourself.
- **Put yourself first:** no, it's not selfish, no, it doesn't mean you are a bad person or unlikeable. It's OK to put yourself first and think about what you really want and need. If you don't, you simply cannot have real relationships with people. If you adopt a doormat mentality, or a Nice Person Mindset (as in Chapter 1), you will not really be true to yourself. Putting yourself first means that you can negotiate with others from a position of strength, where you can say 'no' when things don't suit you. I am not advocating narcissism or selfishness as a 'me, me, me' credo — of course we all have to come second sometimes, especially if we have children. But if you are someone caught up in the Disease to Please, then you will have to

learn to put yourself first. Who knows, you might even get to like doing it in time.

- **Love yourself unconditionally:** we can spend a great deal of time criticising ourselves. If you don't learn to love yourself, then other people will not be able to love you. Nobody loves or likes someone who is constantly down on themselves. It is very irritating to tell someone you like them and they reply, 'Yes, but I'm a terrible person really.' You have to learn to take compliments (as well as give them) and to love yourself for having faults, being imperfect, being human. Love yourself and others will be able to love you; love yourself and you will be able to say 'no'.

- **Let go:** stop being a control freak. Stop trying to make everyone do what you want or see things the way you do. You may be a Happy Helper because you think everyone else should be (goody-two-shoes mentality); you may say 'yes' and expect everyone else to, too. Well, everyone is different. Let go of trying to control people or the outcome of situations. Accept that things happen beyond your control. Let life come to you and be open to it. Your confidence will build as you are able to deal with things and people as they are.

To recap about Step 3 in giving up the Disease to Please, your confidence will build if you can:

- accept yourself;
- love yourself;
- put yourself first;
- let go.

Being confident in yourself: Rene's story

I interviewed a wonderful woman called Rene, who was the first woman firefighter in Bermuda, and who had brought up two children single-handedly from the age of sixteen (when she left Bermuda for London). She had worked extremely hard for the past twenty years, often doing three jobs at once, to keep things together. She'd turned her hand to anything — firefighting, building construction, print and radio journalism, short story writing, teaching, book-keeping, you name it — and had put her children through private education and done a degree herself. Sometimes she worked 110-hour weeks, including night shifts, just to keep everyone happy and alive (she also supported her sister).

However, at the age of thirty-five, with her children now off her hands at university, Rene has learned a lot of hard lessons about life and has finally decided to put herself first. Her confidence has been built through dint of tough experience: 'I have been pulled in many directions and I still am,' explains Rene, 'but I have learned I have to prioritise. It's now time for me. You have to do what you really have to do for yourself, not what everybody expects you to do. You have to do what you need to do for you. That's not selfish, it's real. I now stop and say, "Sorry, I can't do that for you," instead of being everybody's saviour.' Rene has told her sister she needs her to support herself from now on, and has also made sure her children are well provided for now they are independent in full-time education (they've both won scholarships). She has decided to go back to Bermuda and go for achieving her wildest dream: writing a novel. Rene is confident, well-balanced and her own woman because she has now taken time to put herself first, and as a consequence can say 'no' where she would have said 'yes' automatically before.

What difference would it make if you accepted and loved yourself completely? What would it feel like to put yourself first? What would you need to let go of to do that? How would it feel to be confident in the knowledge that you are completely fine, even if you are imperfect? This is Step 4 on your road to recovery from the Disease to Please. Jot down your first thoughts in your notebook for future reference.

Knowing what you want

We can easily become 'yes' men and women if we don't know what we want in life for ourselves. You can become like a fine feather, floated in any direction by the wind, simply because you haven't decided which way you are going. Someone offers you something or asks you to do something and you say, 'Yeah, why not?' Are you choosing? Or is it just a reaction to something being placed in front of you? Drifting is fine - for feathers, teenagers, even twenty-somethings - but by the time you reach your thirties you ought to be in the driving seat in your own life. I don't mean you ought to be a dot.com millionaire YouTube star or married with kids, but I do mean you ought to be pursuing your life goals because, after all, you only have one life and it would be a bit of a shame to waste it. Plus, the less you know about what you want, the more you can fill up your life with doing things for others - so knowing what you want can be a great antidote to the Disease to Please.

How can you know what you really want? You need to take time out to think about your life and where it is going. Also to assess your skills, your abilities, your education, your experience, your wildest dreams and your ability to relate and work with people. Ask yourself: what do I really want out of my life? If there is a resounding silence echoing back, you might find it helpful to talk to a counsellor or life coach, who could help you think in a more focused way about yourself (see Useful contacts). This is especially important if you feel you are at a dead end, doing a boring job, have underachieved, or are in a marriage or relationship which is going nowhere. You might be tempted to have children to fill the emptiness, but on the whole it is a good idea to have children once you know who you are and where you are going, otherwise the job of parenthood will be an utter nightmare (and it wouldn't be much good for the children, either).

Step 5, or knowing what you want, can be aided by doing the following:

- **Become separate from your parents and family of origin:** this doesn't mean rejecting them, but it does mean separating from them physically, emotionally and psychologically. Look at their life and lifestyle. Is that what you want? Or do you want something different? Do you want to be like them or do you want something else? If so, what is it? Allow yourself freedom to dream, to think, to articulate your feelings and ideas. You may not want to follow in their footsteps, or-you may. Fine, if it is your choice, but if you say 'yes' to taking over the family business or having children because it is expected of you, you may not be living your own life, but rather living a life so your parents can enjoy it vicariously. You might also be rebelling against your parents by doing the complete opposite of what they want you to do. Ask yourself, is this a choice or a reaction against their expectations? All this links back to building your confidence, as you have to put yourself first, and you need to let go of family obligation, duty and guilt.

- **Set your own life goals:** allow yourself to think widely about what you want in your life. It may not be possible to be an astronaut or a pop star or to scale Everest, but many things are more within your grasp than you think. Many people are dissatisfied with the jobs they have ended up with or the partners they have settled for. You don't have to settle for less, but you do have to think about what you want for yourself and pursue it actively. Don't be a passive moaner about your life: be an active go-getter, deciding what you want, and go and get it. Even if you fall short of the mark you aim for you will probably get further than if you hadn't tried at all.

- **Grow up:** stop expecting someone else to sort everything else out for you. Adopt the attitude and behaviour of a grown up. Your life is in your hands, only you can take responsibility for you. No one else is responsible for the shape your life takes or the decisions you make or the actions you take. Yes, things will happen - accidents, crises, unforeseen events. It comes down to how you handle what life throws at you. If you can act like a grown up by finding out and pursuing what you want, then you will be in a far stronger position to resist and recover from the Disease to Please.

Emotional literacy

Feelings are feelings, and they are there for a reason (as we saw in Chapter 4). Step 6 is about learning to recognise, feel, accept and work with your feelings, and you will be much more in charge of your life. People who deny their true feelings end up very distorted and unreal. People-pleasers in particular flatten out their wants, needs and desires and, instead, lavish on others what they would really like for themselves (while denying it for themselves). This means you'll need to straighten out emotionally if you want to live free of the Disease to Please, and these simple steps could help you on your way:

- **Accept your feelings:** learn to recognise your feelings and accept them as part of being human. Don't run away from difficult or 'bad' feelings, learn to work with them.
- **Allow your feelings space in your life:** cry when you need to, acknowledge and handle your anger, notice when you're bored. Everyday addictions are an attempt to blot out feelings, and if you can allow yourself to be a sentient person you will gain in strength and power. For more on this see my book *Overcoming Addiction* (Acorn Publishing Ltd, 2018; Amazon).
- **Handle your own and others' emotions:** if you can learn to 'read' your emotions and other people's, you will not be pulled into agreeing with things when you don't want to, nor will you acquiesce to keep the peace. If they get angry, they get angry — that's their feelings; if they try to guilt-trip you, it won't work, because you will be able to analyse what is going on. In terms of emotional literacy, understanding how feelings work will enable you to build appropriate psychological boundaries. This kind of knowledge is power.

Become your true self

Here is the final step - Step 7 - towards becoming your true
self. This is not just one step, but an ongoing process, which
may take months, years, even the rest of your life. It is not a
quick fix, but it is something you can work at over time. It is
inevitable that as you give up the Disease to Please you will
have times of backsliding. There will be moments when you
say 'yes' and then think, 'Damn, why did I say that?' There
will be people who stomp on you, and you let them, and later
you may feel, 'Hell, why did I let them do that?'
    Stop.
    Take a moment.
    Think for a minute.
    Step 7 involves the following:

- **Accept you will make mistakes:** you are human, you're
  not a machine. You will inevitably slip back and make
  mistakes, no matter how hard you try. Accept this is part
  of the process. You can backtrack by noticing what has
  happened. You can go back to someone and say, 'You
  know I agreed to organise the community street party?
  Well, I wasn't thinking about all my commitments at the
  time. Could we discuss it again?' You can decide to go
  ahead this time, and learn your lesson for next time. Or
  you can go back and renegotiate your position: 'You know
  I said I'd pay for the curtains? Well, I'll have to ask you to
  go halves with me. I've had a good look at my finances and
  it would be better for me if we could split it.' It might be
  a bit embarrassing, you may have a bit of a tussle with the
  other person or people, but you can go back and correct
  things if you want to. Accepting you're human - and
  therefore fallible - is the most important thing here.
- **Take time to think:** over and over and over again you
  will feel railroaded into saying 'yes'. Give yourself the
  time you need to think. Thinking goes on all the time
  in our unconscious minds. Give yourself a break and
  your thinking will emerge all on its own. You might find

decisions emerge in dreams and daydreams - note them down if they do. Pay attention to yourself and trust the process.

- **Enjoy your life:** learn to meditate and tune in with your feelings. Take time out from your busy schedule for a walk or to garden, do some exercise, paint a picture, take some photos, play with children, see a film, listen to music, have fun with friends, make love and enjoy solitude. If you put your attention in the present, and stay in touch with yourself, and enjoy whatever you do as much as you can, you will be in a far better position to turn things down if you don't want to do them. You will be in a position of choosing, of being your true and authentic self.
- **Doormat no more:** you no longer have to please and appease to give your life meaning. You and only you are at the centre of your life, and that is as it should be. Give up being a doormat and you will gain in stature and grace. You will be well on your way to becoming your true self, even if you have no idea, right now, what that might be.

To recap, to live free of the Disease to Please:

Step 1:   give up the Four 'Yes' Hooks;
Step 2:   choose when to say 'yes';
Step 3:   build your self-confidence;
Step 4:   accept yourself completely;
Step 5:   know what you want - and go for it;
Step 6:   become emotionally literate;
Step 7:   become your true self.

Power of decision

At the beginning of this book I suggested a mantra against power-lessness, because it reminds you of who is in the driving seat in your life. Not your mum or dad, your boss or partner, your friend or sister. YOU.

It's my life, I'm in charge, and I can decide what I want to do, with whom and when.

This is a great thing to say to yourself when you are drawn to say 'yes' instead of 'no'; it's a wonderful thing to take a moment to remember when you feel you want to run away, instead of confronting someone who is expecting you to be a doormat. You can remember and act on the knowledge:

It's my life, I'm in charge, and I can decide what I want to do, with whom and when.

Repeat daily, morning, noon and night, and who knows, you may well be living completely free of the Disease to Please sooner than you think.

You have only one life, after all.

Isn't it time you lived it to the full?

Just for you...

Useful contacts

Counselling and therapy

BACP (British Association of Counselling and Psychotherapy)
15 St Johns Business Park
Lutterworth
Leicestershire, LE17 4HB
01455 883300
www.bacp.co.uk

Counselling Directory
Counselling Directory, Building 3
Riverside Way, Camberley
Surrey, GU15 3YL
0333 325 2500
www.counselling-directory.org.uk

The Gestalt Centre
15-23 St. Pancras Way
London, NW1 OPT
020 7383 5610
www.gestaltcentre.org.uk

Samaritans
116 123
jo@samaritans.org
www.samaritans.org
jo@samaritans.org

UK Council for Psychotherapy
America House, 2 America Square
London EC3N 2LU
020 7014 9955
www.psychotherapy.org.uk

Relationship Counselling

Relate
Various Locations
0300 100 1234
www.relate.org.uk

Lone Parents

Families Need Fathers
134 Curtain Road
London, EC2A 3AR
0300 0300 110
Helpline: 0300 0300 363
www.fnf.org.uk
fnf@fnf.org.uk

Gingerbread (Formerly the National Council for One Parent Families)
www.gingerbread.org.uk
520 Highgate Studios
53-79 Highgate Road
London, NW5 1TL
020 7428 5400
www.gingerbread.org.uk

Young Minds (Parents' Information Service)
0808 802 5544
www.youngminds.org.uk

Family

Al-Anon Family
57B Great Suffolk Street
London, SE1 0BB
020 7403 0888

Association for Family Therapy and Systemic Practice in the UK
7 Executive Suite, St James Court
Wilderspool Causeway
Warrington
Cheshire, WA4 6PS
01925 444414
www.aft.org.uk

Families Anonymous
The Doddington and Rollo Community Association
Charlotte Despard Avenue
London, SW1 5JE
020 7498 4680
www.famanon.org.uk
office@famanon.org.uk

National Family Mediation
Civic Centre, Paris Street
Exeter, EX1 1JN
0300 4000 636
www.nfm.org.uk

Co-dependency

CODA – Co-dependents Anonymous
www.coda-uk.org
enquiries@coda-uk.org

NACOA (National Association for Children of Alcoholics)
PO Box 64
Bristol, BS16 2UH
Helpline: 0800 358 3456
helpline@nacoa.org.uk

Promis
Various Locations
020 7581 8222
www.promis.co.uk
enquiries@promisclinics.com

Release
Fergusson House, 5th Floor 124 -128 City Road London, EC1V 2NJ
ask@release.org.uk
020 7324 2989
www.release.org.uk
ask@release.org.uk

General Help

Inform (Information Network Focus On Religious Movements)
Houghton Street
Aldwych
London WC2A 2AE
020 7955 7654
www.inform.ac

Further reading

Codependency

Choicemaking: For Co-Dependents, Adult Children and Spirituality Seekers by Sharon Wegscheider (Health Communications, 1985)

Co-Dependence: Misunderstood-Mistreated by Anne Wilson Schaef (Harper & Row, 1986)

Codependent No More: How to Stop Controlling Others and Start Caring for Yourself by Melody Beattie (Harper/ Hazelden, 1990)

Codependency: How to Break Free and Live Your Own Life by David Stafford and Liz Hodgkinson (Piatkus, 1999)

Facing Codependence: What It Is, Where It Comes From, How It Sabotages Our Lives by Pia Mellody, Andrea Wells Miller and J. Keith Miller (Harper & Row, 1989)

Family Intervention: Ending the Cycle of Addiction and Co-Dependency by Frank Picard (Prentice Hall, 1991)

Women and addiction

Love Coach: No-One's Ever Shown You How to Make Love Work Until Now by Susan Quilliam (Thorsons, 2000)

Overcoming Addiction: Positive Steps for Breaking Free of Addiction and Building Self-Esteem by Corinne Sweet (Piatkus, third edition, 2001; Acorn Publishing Ltd, 2019)

Women, Sex and Addiction by Charlotte Davis Kasl (Mandarin, 1989)

Women Who Love Too Much by Robin Norwood (Arrow, 1986)

Stand Your Ground: A Woman's Guide to Self-Preservation by Kaleghl Quinn (Orbis, 1983)

Confidence-building

Be Your Own Life Coach: How to Take Control of Your Life and Achieve Your Wildest Dreams by Fiona Harrold (Hodder & Stoughton, 2000)

The Confidence to Be Yourself: How to Boost Your Self-Esteem by Brian Roet (Piatkus, 1998)

How to Live the Life You Love and Love the Life You Live by James Gladwin (Bene Factum Publishing, 2000)

Irresistibility: Secrets of Selling Yourself by Philippa Davies (Hodder & Stoughton, 2000)

The Nice Factor Book: Are You Too Nice for Your Own Good? by Robin Chandler and Jo Ellen Grzyb (Simon & Schuster, 1997)

Positive Living: The Complete Guide to Positive Thinking and Personal Success by Vera Peiffer (Piatkus, 2001)

The Power of Negative Thinking by Tony Humphreys (Newleaf, 1996)

What Can I Say? Finding the Right Words in Difficult Situations by Sheila Dainow (Piatkus, 1999)

Printed in February 2023
by Rotomail Italia S.p.A., Vignate (MI) - Italy